# WWIII

## REX JONES

WESTBOW
P R E S S
A DIVISION OF THOMAS NELSON

WestBow Press books may be ordered through booksellers or by contacting:

WestBow Press
A Division of Thomas Nelson
1663 Liberty Drive
Bloomington, IN 47403
www.westbowpress.com
1-(866) 928-1240

ISBN: 978-1-4497-1939-5 (sc)

Library of Congress Control Number: 2011932728

Printed in the United States of America

WestBow Press rev. date: 6/27/2011

# DEDICATION

This book is dedicated, to all, who desire to learn from God's word, not that I'm that smart, but what the Lord has shown me, I'm obligated to pass on to others, since God called me to teach his word, 1976, that has been my desire, to teach others, about God's holy word, I stayed up, Many nights, until two, or three, in the morning, with a good Reference Bible, studying God's word, and sleep until it was time to go to work, never missing any sleep, for God's word kept me excited, my desire was to learn all I possibly could, now in 2011, I'm still learning about God's word, and I pray, that I'll never stop learning, for no one will ever know it all, until, they reach, that heavenly Place, with the Lord Jesus Christ, in Glory. ***May God Bless you the Reader***

Evangelist and Teacher, God called, Rex Jones

# CONTENTS

# Introduction

Why I wrote this book, first of all, the Lord called me to teach his word, in the year of 1976, and with thirty five years of study of God's word, God placed in my mind to teach others of what I'd learned, not that I'm all that Smart, but it is my duty to show others, what the Lord has shown me, for these thirty five years.

This is a book about a subject, that I've never heard about, from any scholars, and I've studied after a few, but I had heard about Armageddon, and the final war after the reign of Christ, and even some have read ***Ezekiel, 38, and 39***, and have placed it as the battle of Armageddon, but that was not right, for one simple factor, and that factor, is, that in the battle of Armageddon, and the last war, when God rains down from heaven, fire and brimstone, on the final enemy, both it and Armageddon, both, totals of the armies that come against, the Lord, are completely destroyed, completely wiped out, but the war spoken of in ***Ezekiel 38, 39***, there is the factor, of ***1/6$^{th}$*** of the attacking army get's to return home, and in Armageddon, none remains, to go back home, as well as after the reign of Christ, none get to return back to their home, so since that fact has been known, then this is a completely different war, it has never happened as yet, but according to God's word, it will happen immediately after the church is called out of this world, and the person that wins this war, fulfills some of God's word, he becomes the false Messiah, and he is called the Beast, or Anti-christ, the son of Perdition etc.

The Lord wouldn't let me write this book until, the appointed time, and I believe it points to the time appointed for the Lord to step out on that cloud, and call his children home, now I don't know when that will be, neither does any other, man, because that is God's secret, but according to the word of God, and the happenings in this world, It could be any time now, but the wars, and rumors of wars, and the Earthquakes in divers places, seem to be a fulfilling of the time, when the Lord will call out his children.

I've read after some good men, who are, and were studied men, of great faith, and none that I have read after, ever mentioned that Ezekiel, was speaking of a third world war, that would take place, it seems that the Lord has hid the meaning from the eyes of a lot of men, now I don't know this to be true, but it is strange, that no bible scholars, that I have read after, ever mentioned a third world war.

And again, I'm not trying to make me look so intelligent, but God used a donkey to teach a lesson to his Prophet Baalam, and he used a rooster to speak to the apostle Peter who was another of his prophets, so the Lord can use whatever, or whoever to get his message across.

And If God can use a donkey, and a rooster, surely he can use me.

That is why I have written this short book, on World War Three, so read and hopefully you will learn something, something that you haven't thought of before.

May God Bless you the reader.

# WW111—or—Nuclear War— World War Three

By Evangelist/ & Teacher—Rex Jones Jan/2010

There are three wars mentioned, in the bible, just about everyone has heard of Armageddon, and Hollywood has even made a movie about it, then after the reign of Christ, there is a time, when Satan is loosed, and goes to the four Quarters of the earth, and gathers an army, with the intention, of defeating, the Lord, but God the Father rains down on this army, and destroys all, with hail of fire and brimstone, and totally destroys this army, but the war, that most people have never heard of, happens just after the Rapture of the church, and the purpose of it on God's side is to put into power the Beast, or Anti-christ, for he is the strong Delusion, that God has promised to all, who reject the calling of the Lord for the salvation of the soul, *2ⁿᵈ Thessalonians 2:9-12*, and yes God could speak the word, and it would happen, but to fulfill his word, he's going to let the anti-christ, save Israel, and the majority of the world will declare he is the Messiah, that Israel has been looking for, so long, promised in the Old Testament, the Messiah would come. Ezekiel, the Prophet of God, at that time, and only God could know that this would happen, so he revealed it to, Ezekiel, now notice this war that God showed Ezekiel, *is not* the war of Armageddon, *neither is it* the war after the reign of Christ, on this earth, because according to God's word, both times, the total of each army, that comes against

1

the nation of Israel, will be completely wiped out, at Armageddon, the Lord Jesus will wipe out completely this army that comes against Israel . The same after the 1000 year reign of Christ. And also it is told in

*Revelation 20:7—10,—[7]* *"And when the thousand years are expired, Satan shall be loosed out of his prison,"*
*[8]* *"And shall go out to deceive the nations which are in the four quarters of the earth, Gog and Magog, to gather them together to battle: the number of whom is as the sand of the sea." (Gog, is the devil, Magog, is Russia)*
*[9]* *"And they went up on the breadth of the earth, and compassed the camp of the saints about, and the beloved city: [Jerusalem] and fire came down from God out of heaven, and devoured them."*
*[10]* *"And the devil that deceived them was cast into the lake of fire and brimstone, where the beast and the false prophet are, and shall be tormented day and night for ever and ever."*

*Matthew 24:29—31—[29]* *"Immediately after the tribulation of those days shall the sun be darkened, and the moon shall not give her light, and the stars shall fall from heaven, and the powers of the heavens shall be shaken:"*
*[30]* *"And then shall appear the sign of the Son of man in heaven: and then shall all the tribes of the earth mourn, and they shall see the Son of man coming in the clouds of heaven with power and great glory." (To fight the battle of Armageddon)*
*[31]* *"And he shall send his angels with a great sound of a trumpet, and they shall gather together his elect from the four winds, from one end of heaven to the other."*

This is a time when the seven year tribulation period will have ended, and the Lord will take over, and at this time the anti-christ, or as the word of God says, the Beast, and the false prophet are cast alive into the lake of fire, and the Lord and his armies from the Third Heaven will have come down to rescue Israel, and the remnant of other nations, Egypt, and Assyria, and he will destroy the armies of the beast and the false prophet,

# CHAPTER TWO

# THE WAR OF ARMAGEDDON

_Isaiah 63:1—6—[1]_ "WHO is this that cometh from Edom, with dyed garments from Bozrah? This that is glorious in his apparel, traveling in the greatness of his strength? I that speak in righteousness, mighty to save."
[2] "Wherefore art thou red in thine apparel, and thy garments like him that treadeth in the winefat?"
[3] "I have trodden the winepress alone; and of the people there was none with me: for I will tread them in mine anger, and trample them in my fury; and their blood shall be sprinkled upon my garments, and I will stain all my raiment."
[4] "For the day of vengeance is in mine heart, and the year of my redeemed is come."
[5] "And I looked, and there was none to help; and I wondered that there was none to uphold: therefore mine own arm brought salvation unto me; and my fury, it upheld me."
[6] "And I will tread down the people in mine anger, and make them drunk in my fury, and I will bring down their strength to the earth."

Then we go to————————————————-.

_Revelation 20:4-6—[4]_ "And I saw thrones, and they sat upon them: and I saw the souls of them that were beheaded(the 144,000

3

*Preachers, sealed in Revelation 7ʰ chapter) for the witness of Jesus, and for the word of God, and which had not worshipped the beast, neither his image, neither had received his mark upon their foreheads, or in their hands; and they lived and reigned with Christ a thousand years."*
*[5] "But the rest of the dead lived not again until the thousand years were finished. This is the first resurrection."*
*[6] "Blessed and holy is he that hath part in the first resurrection: on such the second death hath no power, but they shall be priest of God and of Christ, and shall reign with him a thousand years."*

These are the 144,000, preachers, plus the remnants of Egypt Israel, and Assyria, and will live and reign with Christ a thousand years, this is the total of people that will be saved, during the seven years of the Great Tribulation period, total amount 4,320,000 people that will be saved during the great tribulation, to find this answer you go to ***Isaiah,6:13, plus***, ***Revelation 14:1-5, plus Isaiah 19:19-25,*** but the bible says that the number in ***Revelation 7:9,*** came out of great tribulation, well this number also came out of great tribulation, every child of God can tell you, that they have great tribulation, if they have a work to do for Jesus Christ, for the devil is doing everything he can to try to get you to quit, and just give up.

***Revelation 7:9*** has be misinterpreted, misunderstood by a lot of good folks, but when John saw them, he was looking into heaven, and looking on the earth during the time of the Great Tribulation, beside this number that no man could number, of every nation, every tongue, could only be the church, and the Old testament Saints, and the church had already been at the judgement seat of Christ, where they had been rewarded, for they all had on their white robes.

Then we come back to ***Matthew 24:,*** when all the people of the earth will see the Lord coming in power and great glory.

***Matthew 24: 30, 31—[30] "And then shall appear the sign of the Son of man in heaven: and then shall all the tribes of the earth mourn, and they shall see the Son of man coming in the clouds of heaven with power and great glory." (He comes to set up, the judgment of nations)***

*[31] "And he shall send his angels with a great sound of a trumpet, and they shall gather together his elect from the four winds, from one end of heaven to the other."*

His elect, at this time is the remnant of Israel, also the remnant of Egypt, and Assyria. This happens seven years after the rapture of the church, and no, the church will not have to go through the time of the great tribulation, because God has promised us this fact, and you can find this promise in the book of the——————————,

*Revelation 3:10 "Because thou hast kept the word of my patience, I will also keep thee from the hour of Temptation, which shall come upon all the world, to try them that dwell upon the earth."*

Another place you can find this promise, of the church not going through the time of the Great Tribulation period is in

*1ˢᵗ Thessalonians 5:9 "For God hath not appointed us to wrath, but to obtain salvation by our Lord Jesus Christ,"*

And it is for sure, that the Time of the Great Tribulation period, is a time of the wrath of the devil, and the beast, as well as the time of the wrath of God, on wicked mankind.

The following is speaking of the time of the resurrection of the Remnant of Israel, as well as the remnant of Egypt, and the remnant of Assyria.

*Revelation 14:14-16—[14] "And I looked, and behold a white cloud, and upon the cloud one sat like unto the Son of man, having on his head a golden crown, and in his hand a sharp sickle."*
*[15] "And another angel came out of the temple, crying with a loud voice to him that sat on the cloud, Thrust in thy sickle, and reap: for the time is come for thee to reap; for the harvest of the earth is ripe."*
*[16] "And he that sat on the cloud thrust in his sickle on the earth ; and the earth was reaped."*

This speaks of the harvest of the remnant, of Israel, the remnant of Egypt, and the remnant of the Assyrians, at the end of the Seven years of the Great Tribulation period, just before Armageddon, when the Lord gathers his people out of the world, and this is not the church, for the church was Raptured seven years before, this is the tribulation saints of God, that are harvested at this time. and Immediately, the battle of Armageddon, takes place, when the armies of the world gather together, to make war with the Son of God, and his army.

**_Revelation, 3^rd chapter, verse 10_**, and one of the reasons that people don't know this, is that they don't study the book of Revelation, for they think that, it is a dark book, a book of symbols, and can't be understood, but according to God's word, it can be understood, for it is a book of revealing.

That is what the word Revelation, means, Revealing something. Now in the year of our Lord, 2011, it is getting set up, to fulfill, the prophesy of Ezekiel, that God gave to him, for two main, forces are involved at this time, in a small scale war, which will cause the war, that brings about, the Beast, or Anti-christ, to gain his hold on the world, and these two forces, are Israel, and Hammas, as well as parts of Syria, are involved, not the nation, but Terrorist, that take safe harbor there, and the United Nations has already condemned the nation of Israel, because, they are against Israel, because the devil hates Israel, and the UN. Is controlled by the devil. It is for sure also, that God will keep the remnant of Israel from his wrath, as well as those from Egypt, and Assyria.

**_Isaiah 16:4_** **_"Let mine outcasts dwell with thee, Moab; be thou a covert to them from the face of the spoiler: for the extortioner is at an end, the spoiler ceaseth, the oppressors are consumed out of the land."_**

The beast will take over all the world, all except Moab, Ammon and Edom, and all three of these countries are found in the country of modern day Jordan, and God tells what nations that escapes the hands of the beast, [anti-christ] found in, **_Daniel 11:41_** **_"He shall enter also into the glorious land, [Israel] and many countries shall be overthrown: but these shall escape out of his hand, even Edom, and Moab, and the chief of the children of Ammon."_**

God's children, the remnant of Israel, and the remnant of Egypt, and Assyria, will be hid from the wrath of the devil, and the wrath of God, during the last half of the seven years of great Tribulation.

*Matthew 24:15-22—[15]* *"When ye therefore shall see the abomination of desolation, spoken of by Daniel the prophet, stand in the holy place, (whoso readeth, let him understand:"*

This happens in the middle of the great tribulation period, and the Lord Jesus warns Israel to run to the mountains when they see this take place, it is when the Anti-christ, declares himself to be, the Messiah, and demand people of the world to worship him.

*[16]* *"Then let them which be in Judaea flee into the mountains:"* *(Mountains of modern day Jordan)*
*[17]* *"Let him which is on the housetop not come down to take any thing out of his house:"*
*[18]* *"Neither let him which is in the field return back to take his clothes."*
*[19]* *"And woe unto them that are with child, and to them that give suck in those days!"*
*[20]* *"But pray ye that your flight be not in the winter, neither on the sabbath day."*
*[21]* *"For then shall be great tribulation, such as was not since the beginning of the world to this time, no, nor ever shall be."*
*[22]* *"And except those days should be shortened, there should no flesh be saved: but for the elect's sake those days shall be shortened."*

This story is truth, not fiction, there's been too many stories written that were fiction, and imaginary event, or events, and was supposed to be something, that could be backed up by the bible, and I wish you to know, that God has nothing to do with fiction, except to punish it, because it might be an adventure, to some, but it amounts to lies in the name of the Lord, everything that I write to you in this story will be the truth, and will be according to God's word, not my word, but God's word. After this, the anti-christ, we will refer to as the ***Beast***. And If I have to put in a guess, I will let you know. It is My Opinion, and not a proven fact, at least by me. The reason that I give you God's word, is, because you and I can depend upon God's word to be the absolute truth, I don't want to tell you something that I can't back up with God's word, that way I won't get in trouble with the Lord. There is fighting in the middle east, and the UN, has already denounced Israel, as if Israel started the trouble, but Israel didn't start it, it was started when Hammas begin shelling Israel, with rockets, that they got from either North Korea, or from Iran, or Russia, and the terrorists that has found sanctuary in Syria, are also fighting Israel, and the UN, has not condemned, Hammas, nor the terrorists in Syria, but to them Israel is to blame. Because the UN, is controlled by the devil, who hates Israel, and therefore the UN, hates Israel. (if I repeat something, it is because I want to express a certain point)

**_Zechariah 12:3_** *"And in that day will I make Jerusalem a burdensome stone for all people: all that burden themselves with it shall be cut to pieces though all the people of the earth be gathered together against it."*

There will be a war, that will take place after the church is called out of this world, but it will happen almost Immediately, after the Rapture of the church. This is how the beast gets the attention of the whole world, and the world will think that he is the Messiah, for they will think that only God could destroy this great army, led by Russia, that comes against Israel.

And he is that strong delusion, that God promised he would send, to all that reject, or put off too long to accept, the Lord Jesus Christ as their Saviour.

**_2nd Thessalonians 2:8-12—[8]_** *"And then shall that Wicked be revealed, (Beast) whom the Lord shall consume with the spirit of his mouth, and shall destroy with the brightness of his coming:"*
*[9] "Even him, whose coming is after the working of Satan with all power and signs and lying wonders,"*
*[10] "And with all deceivableness of unrighteousness in them that perish; because they received not the love of the truth, that they might be saved."*

*[11] "And for this cause God shall send them strong delusion, that they should believe a lie:"*
*[12] "That they all might be damned who believed not the truth, but had pleasure in unrighteousness."*

There is pleasure in sin, but the results are too much to bear, if anyone leaves this life, without getting saved, or acquainting themselves with the Lord Jesus, or introducing themselves to the Lord by Confessing that they are lost, and desire him to save them. It may not seem to be very much to worry about, but the devil has had lost men and women to write false bibles, and all agree with the Jehovah's witness bible, the New world Translation, and many of them are such as the following, the New Living Translation, the New International Version, The Revised Standard Version, the New King James Version, and many more which are taken from the same corrupt text, that the devil has had published for the purpose of confusing many people, but if they will read ***Ezekiel 28th Chapter***, they will find that the devil has been destroyed approximately 2,588, years ago, on a mountain, in the middle east. in most of these new versions. Which is a blatant lie of Satan, the devil is alive in the here and now. (These versions agree, that the devil was destroyed, but not the authorized King James ) I will give you two verses out of one of these afore mentioned versions, to show you, and then you can see, where they all are coming from. ***The New International Version.*** ***Ezekiel 28:18, 19—[18]*** *"By your many sins and dishonest trade you have desecrated your sanctuaries. So I made a fire come out of you, and it consumed you and I reduced you to ashes on the ground in the sight of all who were watching ."*
*[19] "All the nations who knew you are appalled at you; you have come to a horrible end and will be no more."*

All the other versions, that I mentioned, before completely agree with the NIV, but the ***Authorized King James Version, and the 1611 King James Version***, says this, about the same devil.
***(Authorized King James Version) Ezekiel 28:18,19—[18]*** *"Thou hast defiled thy sanctuaries by the multitude of thine iniquities, by the iniquity of thy traffick; therefore will I bring forth a fire*

*from the midst of thee, it shall devour thee, and I will bring thee to ashes upon the earth in the sight of them that behold thee." (This is to happen in the future.)*
*[19] "All they that know thee among the people shall be astonished at thee: thou shalt be a terror, and never shalt thou be any more."*

The 1611 King James Version says this—

*Ezekiel 28: 18, 19—18] "Thou hast defiled thy sanctuaries by the multitude of thine iniquities, by the iniquitie of thy traffique: therefore will I bring forth a fire from the middest of thee, it shall deuoure thee: and I will bring thee to ashes vpon the earth in the sight of all that behold thee."*
*[19] "All they that know thee among the people, shall be astonished at thee: thou shalt be a terrour, and neuer shalt thou be any more."*

Now don't think that I misspelled, these words here, I didn't, the English words, of the Sixteen hundreds, were spelled different, but they meant the same, if you will notice, the letter U, was used instead of the letter V, and the letter V, was used instead of the letter U, and some of the words were spelled different. But all these two verses of scripture in both the ***1611 King James version,*** and the ***Authorized King James Version***, say the same, that God will destroy the devil in the future, he has not as of yet, for he tempted Jesus, when The Spirit of God led Jesus into the wilderness to be tempted by the devil, in ***Matthew 4:1-11., Mark 1:12, 13., Luke 4:1-13***.

And the devil is here on this earth today, tempting people to do evil, so that means, that these other so-called Versions of the bible, so- called, are lies, And cannot be trusted.

# Chapter Three

# THE RED HORSE AND IT'S RIDER

*Revelation 6:3,4—[3] "And when he opened the second seal, I heard the second beast say, Come and see."*
*[4] "And there went out another horse that was red: and power was given to him that sat thereon to take peace from the earth, and that they should kill one another: and there was given unto him a great sword."*

This was at the time when the apostle John was caught up in the third heaven and looked down upon the earth, and saw these things take place, and when the Son of God opened the second seal of the seven sealed book he saw the second horse revealed, and it's rider, the horse was red, and the old Soviet Union was known as Red, because of it's Communist doctrine, and this horse and rider represent the new Communist doctrine of the new Russian Empire, and don't let anyone fool you, the Old Communist Regime is not finished, it will come back into existence, the former president of Russia, [Putun], is now working to revive the old Soviet Union, and restore the same Communist regime, and it answers to the red horse in *Revelation 6.*

Also it agrees with *Ezekiel 38:1-6.*

*Ezekiel 38:1:—6—[1] "And the word of the LORD came unto me, saying,"*

*[2] "Son of man, set thy face against Gog, the land of Magog, the chief prince of Meshech and Tubal, and prophesy against him."*
*[3] "And say, Thus saith the Lord GOD; Behold, I am against thee, O Gog, the chief prince of Meshech and Tubal."*
*[4] "And I will turn thee back, and put hooks into thy jaws, and I will bring thee forth, and all thine army, horses and horsemen, all of them clothed with all sorts of armour, even a great company with bucklers and shields, all of them handling swords:"*
*[5] "Persia, Ethiopia, and Libya with them; all of them with shield and helmet:"*
*[6] "Gomer, and all his bands, the house of To-gar-mah of the north quarters, and all his bands: and many people with thee."*

God said, Ezekiel, speak against Gog, the land of [Russia] the chief prince of Meshech [Moscow] and Tubal [Tobolisk] and prophesy against him. God said, I will put hooks in the jaws of Russia, and it's allies, and I will bring you and all your army, with all kinds of Armor, every one of them with weapons of war. And as it was in the days of the apostle John, it was the same in the days of the Prophet Ezekiel, a weapon of war was a sword, and the sword in, ***Revelation 6:2,*** is called a great sword, always in God's word a sword symbolizes, a weapon of war, whether it be rifles, bayonets, machine guns, hand grenades, or what ever, tanks, ships, all kinds of arms, and here in ***Revelation*** as well as in ***Ezekiel,*** a sword is a symbol.

If you will notice, who is in this great army, besides the Russian soldiers, soldiers from the old Persian empire, Iran, Afghanistan, Iraq, Pakistan, Turkey, all the descendants of Madai, and the descendants of Javan, spoken of in ***Genesis 10:[2] "The sons of Ja-pheth; Gomer, and Ma-gog, and Ma-dai, and Javan, and Tu-bal, and Me-shech, and Ti-ras."***
*[3] "And the sons of Go-mer; Ashke-naz, and Ri-phath, and To-gar-mah."*
*[4] "And the sons of Ja-van; E-l-shah, and Tar-shish, Kit-tim, and Dod-a-nim."*
*[5] "By these were the isles of the Gentiles divided in their lands; every one after his tongue, after their families, in their nations."*

Ethiopia, a northern African nation, peopled by the descendants of Cush, the son of Ham, the son of Noah, The Libyans, the direct descendants of Lehabim, the son of Mizraim, the son of Cush, the son of Ham, the son of Noah. All of these carrying weapons of war, coming to kill Israelis, Then in verse six of ***Ezekiel 38,*** it says that Gomer, is with them also, Gomer, spoken of in ***Genesis 10,*** as being the son of Japheth, the son of Noah. Gomer is known as the father of all the Celtic nations, such as Germany, Russia, Sweden, Norway, the Dutch, French, British Isles, Ireland, Scotland.

### *"The house of Togarmah, of the north quarters."*

Togarmah, is spoken of as being the son of Gomer, also it is said that the north quarters, always when the word of God speaks of a direction, it is always that direction from Israel, Israel is the most center position in the bible, above is north, right side is, east, left side is west, below Israel, is south, Togarmah settled in the region of Poland, Armenia, and his descendants became a people of Agriculture, breeding of horses, which were sold in ancient Tyre.

***Ezekiel 27:12—14—[12]*** *"Tar-shish was thy merchant by reason of the multitude of all kind of riches; with silver, iron, tin, and lead, they traded. "in thy fairs,"*
*[13] "Ja-van, Tubal, and Meshech, they were thy merchants: they traded the persons of men and vessels of brass in thy market."*
*[14] "They of the house of To-gar-mah traded in thy fair with horses and horsemen and mules."*

This was speaking of the fairs of Tyrus, the ancient city, which was a very wicked city, which boasted of being a city, that was perfect beauty.

***Ezekiel 27:3*** *"And say unto Ty-rus, O thou that art situate at the entry of the sea, (Mediterranean sea) which art a merchant of the people for many isles, Thus saith the LORD God; O Ty-rus, thou hast said, I am of perfect beauty."*

Tyrus the city of evil, was destroyed, in the bottom of the sea. The red horse of ***Revelation 6:2,*** represents a horse of war, and red is the color of Communism, and the mighty army that will come down to Jerusalem, at the very first of the great tribulation period, and will be made up of Russia, and it's satellite nations. Israel is still God's people, even though, according to God's word, they are at this time blinded to the truth of God's word blinded in part, because they cannot accept the Lord Jesus Christ as being the Messiah, that the nation of Israel has looked for all these many years.

Some will try to tell you that communism is dead in Russia, and it's satellite nations, but don't you believe it for one minute, for communism is still very much alive in Russia, as well as these other nations. Saudi Arabia, as well as Spain, must be allied with Russia, at the time of the invasion, for ***Ezekiel 38:13*** says, that Sheba, Dedan, which are descendants of Abraham, through his last wife, Keturah, Sheba and Dedan are grandsons of Abraham, and they, people the land known in bible times as Havilah, modern day name for it is Saudi Arabia. Tarshish, is the biblical name for modern day Spain. And this great army must come close to these two nations, most likely through the Mediterranean Sea, for they ask this great army, ***"Art thou come to take a spoil?"***

***Ezekiel 38: 13 "Sheba, and Dedan, and the merchants of Tarshish, with all the young lions thereof, shall say unto thee, Art thou come to take a spoil? Hast thou gathered thy company to take prey? To carry away silver and gold, to take away cattle and goods, to take a great spoil?"***

Most likely they will come down the Atlantic, enter in the Mediterranean sea, and disembark in the Persian Gulf, World Jealousy, because of the riches of Israel, is one of the great motives of this army, to invade Israel, Russia has always desired the warm ports of Israel, so that they can ship out oil, there, from the middle east. Also Israel has been buying up silver, and gold, besides the natural resources of Israel, as in the dead sea, it is said that the minerals found there, are in untold riches, and these countries want all of this great spoil.

***Ezekiel 38:11,12—[11] "And thou shalt say, I will go up to the land of unwalled villages; I will go to them that are at rest, that***

*dwell safely, all of them dwelling without walls, and having neither bars nor gates."*

First they were coming down, so that means, they were going south to the Persian gulf, then up to Israel, to take great spoil.

*[12] "To take a spoil, and to take a prey; to turn thine hand upon the desolate places that are now inhabited, and upon the people that are gathered out of the nations, which have gotten cattle and goods, that dwell in the midst of the land."* (Israel)

Their idea is, that they are coming to make war with Israel, so they can get great spoil, but God is making them come to make war with Israel, for a purpose, and that purpose is, to get the beast, [anti-christ] in power, God's word will be fulfilled. Because God will work his strong delusion, that he said he would send to those who have heard, or will hear the gospel of Jesus Christ, and reject it, and God said in **2ⁿᵈ _Thessalonians_**, that he would give them a strong delusion, so that they would believe a lie and be damned, who had pleasure in unrighteousness. And the beast, [anti-christ ] is the strong delusion.

**2ⁿᵈ _Thessalonians 2:10-12—[10]_** *"And with all deceivableness of unrighteousness in them that perish; [wasted, lost] because they received not the love of the truth, <u>that they might be saved."</u>*
*11 "And for this cause God shall send them strong delusion, that should believe a lie:"*
*[12] "That they all might be damned who believed not the truth, but had pleasure in unrighteousness."*

There will yet be three different wars, Just after the rapture of the church, or if you don't like the word rapture, ( the calling out of this world, the bride of Christ) then will be the war, that we are speaking of, and God will let man rescue Israel this time, simply to fulfill his word, that the beast be revealed, [anti-christ], because he will win this war, in order to set himself up as being the one who no one can stand against, this great army led by Russia. The difference in this war, and the other two, is in this war 1/6th of this army, will be able to return home.

*Revelation 13:4* "And they worshipped the dragon [devil] which gave power unto the beast: and they worshipped the beast, saying, Who is like unto the beast? Who is able to make war with him."

And many people will accept the mark of the beast, and doom their souls to the lake of fire and Brimstone, as spoken of in *Revelation 20:*

Then there will be a war called Armageddon, in the valley of Meddigo which will be fought, at the end of the seven years of Great Tribulation, and the Lord will destroy completely all of this army, that will come against Israel, at his second stage of the second coming.

*Revelation 19:19-21—[19]* "And I saw the beast, and the kings of the earth, and their armies, gathered together to make war against him that sat on the horse, [Jesus Christ] and against his army."

*[20]* "And the beast was taken, and with him the false prophet that wrought miracles before him, with which he deceived them that had received the mark of the beast, and them that worshipped his image. These both were cast alive into a lake of fire burning with brimstone."

*[21]* "And the remnant {rest of this army] were slain with the sword of him that sat upon the horse, which sword proceeded out of his mouth: [His word] and all the fowls were filled with their flesh."

The war after the reign of Christ, will be when once again Satan will try a last ditch effort to destroy Israel, and prove to the world, that he is stronger than God, but God will rain down from heaven, fire and brimstone, and destroy this army and the devil will be cast into the lake of fire, where the beast, and the false prophet will have been for one thousand years.

*Revelation 20 :7-10—[7]* "And when the thousand years are expired, Satan shall be loosed out of his prison."     (*This is just after the reign of Christ*)

*[8] "And shall go out to deceive the nations which are in the four quarters of the earth, Gog and Ma-gog, to gather them together to battle: the number of whom is as the sand of the sea."*
*[This is the same head-quarters as in the time of <u>Ezekiel 38,39</u>, but the difference is, it's been at least one thousand years, after the time that Ezekiel wrote about, and every one that comes against Israel this time is completely destroyed, not one is left, God destroys them all.]*

Remember the war that Ezekiel wrote about, one sixth of this Russian led army will be left to return home.

<u>*Revelation 20:9,10*</u>—*[9] "And they went up on the breadth of the earth, and compassed the camp of the saints about, and the beloved city: [Jerusalem] and fire came down from God out of heaven, and devoured them." (This will take place, 1000 years after the church is called out)*
*[10] "And the devil that deceived them was cast into the lake of fire and brimstone, where the beast and the false prophet are, and shall be tormented day and night for ever and ever."*

The scripture verses used in this study, are from the Authorized King James bible, and where there is a question, there is an answer, but to find the answer, requires much study, of the same bible, as far as this author is concerned, it is the only bible there is, for it is the preserved, inerrant, infallible, scriptures, and they are from the Antioch preserved manuscripts.

# CHAPTER FOUR

# THE WHITE HORSE AND IT'S RIDER DESTROY THE RED HORSE AND IT'S RIDER!

The white horse here is the answer to the first seal being opened by the Lamb of God, the only one able to look upon and to open the seven sealed book.

*Revelation 5:1—8—[1]* "AND I saw in the right hand of him that sat on the throne [God the Father] a book written within and on the backside, sealed with seven seals."
*[2]* "And I saw a strong angel proclaiming with a loud voice, Who is worthy to open the book, and to loose the seals thereof?"
*[3]* "And no man in heaven, nor in earth, neither under the earth, was able to open the book, neither to look thereon."
*[4]* "And I wept much, because no man was found worthy to open and to read the book, neither to look thereon."
*[5]* "And one of the elders saith unto me, Weep not: behold, the Lion of the tribe of Juda, the root of David, hath prevailed to open the book, and to loose the seven seals thereof."
*[6]* "And I beheld, and, lo, in the midst of the elders, stood a Lamb as it had been slain, having seven horns and seven eyes, which are the seven Spirits of God sent forth into all the earth."

*[7] "And he came and took the book out of the right hand of him that sat upon the throne."*
*[8] "And when he had taken the book, the four beasts and four and twenty elders fell down before the Lamb, having every one of them golden vials full of odours, which are the prayers of saints."*

This scene is in the third heaven, where God's throne is, and John wept much, because there was found no man, in the earth nor under the earth, worthy to open the book, or to look on it., then one of the elders told John not to weep, for the Lion of the tribe of Juda, and the descendant of David, was able to open the book and to break the seals of the book, then John saw a Lamb, the one who died on the cross for the sins of the whole world, Jesus Christ. And he was the only one worthy to open this seven sealed book.

When the Lamb of God, Jesus Christ, started to open the seals of the book, in the sixth chapter of Revelation, then he opened the first seal.

*<u>Revelation 6:1,2—[1]</u> "AND I saw when the Lamb opened one of the seals, and I heard, as it were the noise of thunder, one of the four beast saying, Come and see."*
*[2] "And I saw, and behold a white horse: and he that sat on him had a bow; and a crown was given unto him: and he went forth conquering, and to conquer."*

And when you read this, know this, this is not the Lord Jesus, but a devil made copy, he is the anti-christ, the beast, and he is seen as coming in peace, no arrows, only a bow, he's coming in peace, if he has to kill half the world to accomplish this. The devil always copies what the Lord God does, and it is not a good copy, but a flawed copy, always. He set forth to conquer the world, because he accepts what the devil offered the Lord Jesus, if he would fall down and worship him, but the Lord Jesus turned down all the kingdoms of the world. (For he already owned them, he created them)

*<u>Matthew 4:8-11</u> "Again, the devil taketh him up into an exceeding high mountain, and sheweth him all the kingdoms of the world, and the glory of them:"*

*[9] "And saith unto him, All these things will I give thee, if thou wilt fall down and worship me."*

*[10 "Then saith Jesus unto him, Get thee hence, Satan: for it is written, Thou shalt worship the Lord thy God, and him only shalt thou serve."*

*[11] "Then the devil leaveth him, and, behold, angels came and ministered unto him."*     *[Jesus]*

But the beast will accept all the kingdoms of the world, and he will be thought of, as the Messiah, that was promised to Israel, and two thirds of the nation of Israel will accept him as such, but one third of the nation of Israel will refuse to accept him, as the Messiah.

More on this man on the white horse, with just a bow, no arrows

*Daniel 11:36-45—[36] "And the king shall do according to his will; he shall exalt himself, and magnify himself above every god, and shall speak marvellous things against the God of gods, and shall prosper till the indignation be accomplished: for that that is determined shall be done."*

The anti-christ will accomplish to exalt himself, as god, and it is because the one true God will use him to accomplish his will, God will use the devil's tool to fulfill his word, if you will notice the last phrase in verse 36, *"For that that is determined shall be done."*
*Daniel 11:37 "Neither shall he regard the God of his fathers, nor the desire of women, nor regard any god: for he shall magnify himself above all."*

Now this verse tells us quite a lot about this man, who will be a false god, first of all he will be an Israelite, for it states, *"that he will not regard the God of his fathers."*

Some say that he will be a descendant of Dan, because the descendants of Dan, are not mentioned in the 144,000, but of Manasseh, were sealed twelve thousand in his stead, and it also points to that it will be a descendant of Dan, when Jacob was blessing his sons in—, *Genesis 49:17*

*Genesis 49:16,17-[16]* *"Dan shall judge his people, as one of the tribes of Israel."*
*[17]* *"Dan shall be a serpent by the way, an adder in the path, that biteth the horse heels, so that his rider shall fall backward."*

It doesn't come outright and say, that a descendant of Dan will be the rider on the white horse, but the rider that Jesus reveals, when he opens the first seal, is astride a horse, and in the Blessing of Jacob to his sons, Dan is the only one mentioned with a horse. The beast, or anti-christ, will behead the 144,000, because they are preaching against him, so it would be harder for him to behead, his own tribesmen, or so it would seem. *He will not regard the desire of women* So it would seem that he will be a homosexual person, for he will not regard the desire of women, by that time it will be regarded as something natural, for now they preach that a person is born that way, and there is nothing, he or she can do about it. But God hates it, because it is unnatural, and God said it was an Abomination to him. But the devil wants to be a god, and it will have to be against everything that the true God is for. And the anti-christ will not regard any god, but will exalt himself above every god.

*Daniel 11:38* *"But in his estate shall he honour the God of forces: and a god whom his fathers knew not shall he honour with gold, and silver, and with precious stones, and pleasant things."* (the only God that Israel worshiped was the God of Israel, not another god.)

This also points to him being an Israelite, for he will honor a god his fathers knew not.

And it could be, that he will regard Allah, the Moon god of Arabia, whom the Muslims worship, because his fathers never knew this god, and why not? On *November 7-12/2002,* during Ramadan, President Bush hosted a dinner in honor of Islam and the revelation of God's word in the holy Qur'an, slapping the true God in the face.

*Daniel 11:39,40,—[39]* *"Thus shall he do in the most strong holds with a strange god, whom he shall acknowledge and increase with glory: and he shall cause them to rule over many, and shall divide the land for gain."*

*[40] "And at the time of the end shall the king of the south push against him like a whirlwind, with chariots, and with horsemen, and with many ships; and he shall enter into the countries, and shall overflow and pass over."*

What land will he divide for gain? It could be Israel, even today, the leaders of the US, with the blessings of the United Nations, are dividing Israel to give to the Palestinians, for the cause of Peace, so they say. But there will never be Peace in the Middle East, until the Lord Jesus Christ sets up his Kingdom, then there will be a thousand years of peace.

*Daniel 11:41 "He shall enter also into the glorious land, and many countries shall be overthrown: but these shall escape out of his hand, even Edom and Moab, and the chief of the children of Ammon."*

It states the anti-christ will enter into Israel, for to God it is the glorious land, and he will over throw many countries, for he will exalt his power. But three countries, (Bible time countries) which are now in modern day Jordan, for God has a place picked out, to be a covering for his people, the Remnant of Israel, that will be saved during the time of the Great Tribulation.

*Isaiah 16:4 "Let mine outcasts dwell with thee, Moab; be thou a covert to them from the face of the spoiler:[Anti-christ] for the extortioner is at an end, the spoiler ceaseth, the oppressors are consumed out of the land."*

This happens in the middle of the great tribulation period, when the anti-christ sets himself up to be worshiped, and the remnant of Israel will refuse to worship him.

*Matthew 24:15,16—[15] "When ye therefore shall see the abomination of desolation, spoken of by Daniel the prophet, stand in the holy place, (whoso readeth, let him understand:)"*
*[16] "Then let them which be in Judaea flee into the mountains:"*

This speaks also of the beast, or anti-christ when in the middle of the great tribulation period, declares himself to be a god, and demand worship, and this is also where God tells Moab to be a covert for the remnant of his people. For these three countries are mountainous countries, Edom, Moab, and Ammon.

**_Daniel 11:42_** *"He shall stretch forth his hand also upon the countries: and the land of Egypt shall not escape."*

He will conquer many countries, but these three will escape from his hand, Edom, Moab, and Ammon.

**_Daniel 11:43_** *"But he shall have power over the treasures of gold and of silver, and over all the precious things of Egypt: and the Libyans and the Ethiopians shall be at his steps."*

Egypt will fall to him, as well as Libya, and Ethiopia will be in his complete power.

**_Daniel 11: 44_** *"But tidings out of the east and out of the north shall trouble him: therefore he shall go forth with great fury to destroy, and utterly make away many."*

But news from the east and the north will trouble him, and he will go and destroy many, this is when he destroys the mighty Russian army, no doubt with Nuclear weapons, or perhaps an Hydrogen bomb, and It is my thoughts, that God is preserving the United States for the purpose of supplying the Anti-christ, because God will fulfill his word, if he has to use man to do it. Russia would be from the north, north of Jerusalem, and what is east of Jerusalem? Would it not be the Muslim nations, for their hatred for Israel is known to all the world .Iran has boasted they would blow Israel off the map, and Russia has always wanted the warm ports to ship out the oil they buy from the middle east. And God will have put into his mind, this is the time to get his power over the whole world, and all this will happen just after the rapture of the church, and when he wins this great war, the whole world will worship him, All except 1,440,000 of Israelis, and 1,440,000, Egyptians, and 1,440,000 Assyrians. Total = 4,320,000, souls that will be saved during the time of the great tribulation period. During the seventieth week of God's Calendar

**_Daniel 11:45_** *"And he shall plant the tabernacle of his palace between the seas in the glorious holy mountain;[Israel] yet he shall come to his end, and none shall help him."*

He will come to his end, when the Lord Jesus Christ, defeats him at Armageddon, and throws him and the false prophet into the lake of fire and brimstone. But before that happens to him, he will prove himself to the world, with the help of the false prophet

**_Zechariah 13:8,9—[8]_** *"And it shall come to pass, that in all the land, [Israel] saith the LORD, two parts therein [2/3rds ] shall be cut off and die; but the third [1/3rd ] shall be left therein."*
*[9] "And I will bring the third part through the fire, [the great tribulation] and will refine them as silver is refined, and will try them as gold is tried: they shall call on my name, and I will hear them: I will say, It is my people: and they shall say, The LORD is my God."*

The Lord will come down from the third heaven and gather his Elect from the four quarters of the earth. at this time he will come from the East of Jerusalem, if you were standing on the western side of Jerusalem, you could see him come from the Eastern sky.

The following is the start of this great war, "Iran now wants a nuclear bomb, and has already bragged, that when that happens, they intend to blow Israel off the map, Israel to them is the small Satan, while the USA is the big Satan, so that ought to sound a warning to the USA, and Great Britain, and other free countries, that the Islamic nations all want to rule the world. God predicted this approximately 2,588, years ago, God has predicted a global war, yet government leaders wonder why Iran, Syria, and other Islamic nations, want to destroy Israel, and Ultimately the United States of America.

The Qur'an speaks of killing all infidels, and an Infidel, is simply one who does not believe in the same thing that Muslims do, and that includes Christians and Jews. In the Qur'an, in the book of—

*Surah 9:5* "So when the sacred months have passed away, then slay the idolaters wherever you find them, and take them captives and besiege them and lie in wait for them in every ambush, then if they repent and keep up prayer and pay the poor rate, leave their way free to them; surely Allah is forgiving, merciful."

Does this sound like a peaceful religion? Absolutely not, and this is not the only verse that says to slay the idolaters, or infidels, but there are many passages that states the same. Remember, that an infidel, is one that does not subscribe to the Muslim religion.

The news media is now speaking of perhaps a global war, and it really could be the start of the same war that the prophet Ezekiel speaks of. And it is a war, where the Beast gets his power to rule the world, for the world will wonder after the beast, and say that this has to be God, because man is not capable of defeating this army.

*Revelation 6:1,2—[1]* **"AND I saw when the Lamb opened one of the seals, and I heard, as it were the noise of thunder, one of the four beasts saying, Come and see."**
**[2] "And I saw, and behold a white horse: and he that sat on him had a bow; and a crown was given unto him: and he went forth conquering, and to conquer."**

This war will happen just after the rapture of the church, then when the Holy Spirit, is taken out of this world, then Satan will have a free reign for a short period of time, but long enough to deceive many millions of people. (I personally believe that the Lord is sparing the United States of America, for the one purpose of saving his people Israel, because the USA, is the only nation that has the capability to win this war, and save Israel from destruction, by this great horde of soldiers that will come against Israel), with the intent of completely destroying that nation, and I believe that the USA, will produce the Beast, or Anti-christ! For it is the only country that has the capability to win this war. Many Theologians, and politicians, think the Old Soviet Union, is done away with, and Communism is dead in Russia, but the Soviet Union will come together once more to make up this great army. And you might say that the Lord can destroy this army with just his word, and yes he could, but he's going to let man win this war to fulfill his word, so that the beast can become that strong delusion, that the Lord promised in his word.

*<u>Revelation 13:4</u> "And they worshipped the dragon which gave power unto the beast: and they worshipped the beast, saying, <u>Who is like unto the beast? Who is able to make war against him?</u>*

*<u>John5:43</u> "I am come in my Father's name, and ye receive me not: if another shall come in his own name, him ye will receive." <u>These were the words of Jesus.</u>*

# CHAPTER FIVE

# PEOPLE THAT MAKE UP THIS ARMY, COMING AGAINST ISRAEL AT THIS TIME

*Ezekiel 38 :1—6—[1] "AND the word of the LORD came unto me, saying."*
*[2] "Son of man, set thy face against Gog, the land of Magog, the chief prince of Meshech and Tubal, and prophesy against him."*
*[3] "And say, Thus saith the Lord GOD; Behold, I am against thee, O Gog, the chief prince of Meshech and Tubal:"*
*[4] "And I will turn thee back, and put hooks into thy jaws, and I will bring thee forth, and all thine army, horses and horsemen, all of them clothed with all sorts of armour, even a great company with bucklers and shields, all of them handling swords:"*
*[5] "Persia, Ethiopia, and Lybya with them; all of them with shield and helmet:"*
*[6] Gomer, and all his bands; the house of Togarmah; of the north quarters, and all his bands: and many people with thee."*

Gog, the chief Prince of Magog, and Tubal, is none other than the devil himself., and Magog is Russia, and Meshech, and Tubal, being Moscow, and Toblesk, if you'll remember Noah had three sons, the eldest being <u>*Japheth,*</u> and his eldest son was <u>*(1)Gomer, (2)Magog, and (3) Madai, (4) Javan, (5) Tubal, (6) Meshech, (7) Tiras,*</u> he had seven sons, and after the Lord came down, and scattered the languages of the people, they dispersed to many different parts of the globe, and these sons of Japheth, *(1) Gomer*, the father of the ancient Crimerians from which the Celtic people descended.*(2) Magog*, from him are descended the ancient Scythians which are predominately modern Russians, *(3) Madai*, father of the ancient Medes. *(4) Javan*, father of Grecians, and Syrians *(5) Tubal*, his descendants peopled the region south of the Black sea, and is most likely in Tobolsk, and Tobolsk, perpetrates the tribal name, also a branch of these people went to Spain *(6) Meshech*, Peopled Tubal, Magog, as well as other northern nations, which make up modern day Russia, *(7) Tiras*, the father of the Thracians.Perhaps this will give you a background, on some of the people that make up this vast army that comes against Israel, just after the church is called out of this world, and when the church is called out, the Holy Spirit goes with them, and then the devil has a free reign, at least as much as God allows him to have. All These People that come against Israel, are Germans, Britains, French, Poland, all the old Russian Empire plus many more countries that will ally themselves with Russia, because God has let the devil be in charge, of this world, just so his word will be fulfilled. *The house of Togarmah of the north quarters, and all his bands: and many people with thee."* And according to the word of God, it is the Holy Spirit that is holding back now, the evil, that takes place, during the time of the Great Tribulation period.

*2nd Thessalonians 2:6, 7—[6] "And now ye know what withholdeth that he might be revealed in his time."*
*[7] "For the mystery of iniquity doth already work: only he who now letteth will let, until he be taken out of the way."*

This speaks of the Holy Spirit holding back the beast, or anti-christ, from being revealed, And Russia from starting this war against Israel.

This also tells me, that immediately after the Rapture of the church, is when this Global war starts, and when the Anti-christ get's his authority over the world, by winning this war, rescuing Israel. Now let's go back to *Ezekiel 38,39,* and pick up there.

*Ezekiel 38:7,8—[7]* *"Be thou prepared, and prepare for thyself, thou, and all thy company that are assembled unto thee, and be thou a guard unto them."*

God is warning Russia to be on guard, and to fight for the different people with it, now don't get too excited, for all these things will take place according to God's word.

*[8] "After many days thou shalt be visited: in the latter years thou shalt come into the land that is brought back from the sword, and is gathered out of many people, against the mountains of Israel, which have been always waste: but it is brought forth out of the nations, and they shall dwell safely all of them."*

Now Israel was brought back to it's homeland, in **May 13, 1948.** Which is a small piece of the land that Israel owns, Israel was given land from the Nile river to the Euphrates river, from Southern Turkey - down to the Persian Gulf. All this land was given to Abraham, and down to Isaac, and down to Jacob, and his descendants, no land was given to the Arabs. the descendants of Ishmael. But Great Britain gave to the Arabs, most of the land, that God gave to Abraham, Isaac, Jacob, and gave to Israel, the worst part of the land, and Great Britain, has suffered since, at one time, the saying was, **"The sun never sets on Great Britain"** but not any more, all Great Britain, has now is just a few Islands, Why? Because they went against Israel, and the Promise of blessing and cursing is still at this time, as good as it ever was, if any want to get a hurting, then go against Israel.

*Genesis 25:5,6—[5] And Abraham gave all that he had unto Isaac."*
*[6] "But unto the sons of the concubines, which Abraham had, Abraham gave gifts, and sent them away from Isaac his son, while he yet lived, eastward, unto the east country."*
*Deuteronomy 30:1 "AND it shall come to pass, when all these things are come upon thee, the blessing and the curse, which I have set before thee, and thou shalt call them to mind among all the nations, whither the LORD thy God hath driven thee."*

## Chapter Six

# *BACK TO EZEKIEL 38*

*Ezekiel 38:9,10—[9]* "*Thou shalt ascend and come like a storm, thou shalt be like a cloud to cover the land, thou, and all thy bands, and many people with thee.*"
*[10]* "*Thus saith the Lord GOD; it shall come to pass, that at the same time shall things come into thy mind, and thou shalt think an evil thought.*"

We can all be assured of one thing, the Lord will fulfill, every bit of his word, whether we believe it or not, and I believe the anti-christ will be a United States President, for the US, has the means to destroy this mighty army, that will come down to destroy Israel. Israel is a sore place, in the eyes of most of the world, because most of this world, is controlled by Satan, and he hates Israel, because he hates God, and Israel is still God's people, and always will be God's people, and all who loves Israel, God has promised he would Prosper, so that means, all who hate's Israel will suffer greatly.

*Psalms 122:6* "*Pray for the peace of Jerusalem: they shall prosper that love thee.*"

But the Lord God shall save his people Israel, at whatever cost, because evil will never win, against God's people, for the Lord will rescue Israel from this mighty army, headed up by Russia, and you can be sure, that there will be a remnant of Israel saved, no matter how much the rest of the world hates Israel.

*Psalms 124 :1-8—[1]* *"IF it had not been the LORD who was on our side, now may Israel say;"*
*[2]* *"If it had not been the LORD who was on our side, when men rose up against us:"*
*[3]* *"Then they had swallowed us up quick, when their wrath was kindled against us:"*
*[4]* *"Then the waters had overwhelmed us, the stream had gone over our soul:"*
*[5]* *"Then the proud waters had gone over our soul."*
*[6]* *"Blessed be the LORD, who hath not given us as a prey to their teeth."*
*[7]* *"Our soul is escaped as a bird out of the snare of the fowlers: the snare is broken, and we are escaped."*
*[8]* *"Our help is in the name of the LORD, who made heaven and earth."*

*Zechariah 13:8,9*, says, that two thirds of Israel will accept the mark of the beast, but one third will reject the mark, and in the last three and one half years of the tribulation period, they will be hid by the Lord in the land of Moab, which is in the land of modern day Jordan, which in all reality belongs to Israel, for God has given to Israel, the land from Egypt's Nile river, to the Euphrates river in Iraq, and from southern Turkey, down to the Persian gulf.

Then you can go to the book of Isaiah, and find out just how many people will be saved during the seven years of the great tribulation period.

*Isaiah 6:9—13—[9]* *"And he said, Go, and tell this people, Hear ye indeed, but understand not; and see ye indeed, but perceive not."*
*[10]* *"Make the heart of this people(Israel) fat, and make their ears heavy, and shut their eyes; lest they see with their eyes; and hear with their ears, and understand with their heart, and convert, and be healed."*

*[11] "Then said I, how long? And he answered, Until the cities be wasted without inhabitant, and the houses without man, and the land be utterly desolate,"*

*[12] "And the LORD have removed men far away, (<u>Rapture of the church</u>), and there be a great forsaking in the midst of the land."*

*[13] "But yet in it shall be a tenth, and it shall return, and shall be eaten: as a teil tree, and as an oak, whose substance is in them, when they cast their leaves: so the holy seed shall be the substance thereof."*

One tenth of the remnant of Israel will return to the Lord, during the time of the Great Tribulation Period, and be eaten up by the world, or killed, by the beast, and the holy seed, The Lord Jesus will be the substance of the 144,000 preachers, who will be killed by the beast, because they will be preaching against him, and some people will believe them, not, a large number, but a very small amount of people according to the population of the world.

And the story of a great number that will be saved, during the Great Tribulation Period, is a mis- interpretation of God's word, If one will notice, John saw this great number that no man can number, at the same time he saw the Great Tribulation, and this great number that no man could number, were already before the throne of God, with their White Robes on, meaning they had already been judged at the Judgment seat of Christ, and rewarded for their service on this earth, and this great number could only be the church, and the Old Testament Saints. But you say the Bible states, these are they, that come out of great tribulation, and yes they are, but remember the Old Testament Saints, and the Church has been in great tribulation since Adam and Eve were put out of the Garden of Eden, for the devil has fought, God's saints with great war, on them since, God put a curse on him, and cast him out of heaven, and changed his name to Satan the great red dragon, the devil, etc. for he hates God, and all that God loves.

To find out how many will be saved during the time of the Great Tribulation Period, go to ***Revelation 14:1-5—[1] "AND I looked, and, lo, a Lamb stood on the mount Sion, and with him***

*an hundred forty and four thousand, having his Father's name*
*written in their foreheads."*
*[2] "And I heard a voice from heaven, as the voice of many*
*waters, and as the voice of a great thunder: and I heard the voice*
*of harpers harping with their harps:"*
*[3] "And they sung as it were a new song before the throne, and*
*before the four beasts, and the elders: and no man could learn*
*that song but the hundred and forty and four thousand, which*
*were redeemed from the earth."*
*[4] "These are they which were not defiled with women; for they*
*are virgins. These are they which follow the Lamb whithersoever*
*he goeth. These were redeemed from among men, being the first*
*fruits unto God and to the Lamb."*
*[5] "And in their mouth was found no guile: for they are without*
*fault before the throne of God."*

The 144,000, Israelis that were sealed in ***Revelation 7th Chapter***, are seen here by John, and they are a tenth of Israel that will be saved according to this, as well as according to ***Isaiah 6th Chapter***, notice what they are called here in ***Revelation 14:1-5, "(FIRSTFRUITS")*** Always the Tithe in the Old Testament, is one tenth of the complete harvest, and it is called ***(FIRSTFRUITS)***, so that means the 144,000, is a tenth of the remnant of Israel, that will be saved. So multiply 144,000, by 10, and the answer is 1,440,000, Israelis that will be saved during the Great Tribulation Period., to find the total of people that will be saved during the great tribulation period, go to ***Isaiah 19:20-25*** ———————————————.

***Isaiah 19:20-25—[20] "And it shall be for a sign and for a*** *witness unto the LORD of hosts in the land of Egypt: for they shall cry unto the LORD because of the oppressors, and he shall send them a Saviour, and a great one, and he shall deliver them."*
*[21] "And the LORD shall be known to Egypt, and the Egyptians shall know the LORD in that day, and shall do sacrifice and oblation; yea, they shall vow a vow unto the LORD, and preform it."*

*[22] "And the LORD shall smite Egypt: he shall smite and heal it: and they shall return even to the LORD, and he shall be intreated of them, and shall heal them."*
*[23] "In that day shall there be a highway out of Egypt to Assyria, and the Assyrian shall come into Egypt, and the Egyptian into Assyria, and the Egyptians shall serve with the Assyrians."*
*[24] "In that day shall <u>Israel be the third with Egypt and with Assyria</u>, even a blessing in the midst of the land;"*
*[25] "Whom the LORD of hosts shall bless, saying, Blessed be Egypt my people, and Assyria the work of my hands, and Israel mine inheritance."*

So there shall be, ***1,440,000 Israelis***, and ***1,440,000 Egyptians***, and ***1,440,000 Assyrians*** saved during the time of the Great Tribulation Period. For it states, that Israel will be one third with Egypt and with Assyria, so the total saved will be ***3,420,000*** that will be saved during the time of the Great Tribulation Period. Everyone knows where Egypt is, but the country of Assyria, is found in Iraq, which stretches from southern Turkey down towards ancient Babylon, and narrow strip of land.

Now back to the war that will be at the very first of the Tribulation Period, which will bring the Beast into power, he will defeat this mighty army led by Russia, and people will think that he has to be the Messiah, because only God could do this feat, never a mere man, but will declare that he has to be the Messiah. And will accept his mark, either on their right hand, or in their foreheads, and no one can buy, or sell except they have this mark. People have foolishly predicted it will be Nero, some say it will be the former President of the US. Roland Wilson Reagan, each name has 6 letters in it, so They believe that amounts to 666, and yet some say it will be John F. Kennedy, because he was wounded in the head, but none of these are right, because if any of these are in hell, they will not come back, to back up the devil no matter how much he has to offer, and if they are in heaven, then they will never, ever back up the devil in his evil works.

Now I nor none on earth, know who it will be, for it is a secret of the Lord, and he hasn't informed any man, who it will be, I believe it will be a nuclear war, and the US, is the only country that can defeat this great army, led by Russia, some say it will be a one day war, but it might be a longer war than that, but it will be a quick fought war.

When the LORD opens the seven seals, the first seal, will reveal the beast, and the second seal, reveals Russia, that will take peace from the earth, and has a great sword, or a great weapon, and that great weapon could be a Hydrogen Bomb, that the United States, has to use.

*Revelation 6:3, 4—[3] "And when he had opened the second seal, I heard the second beast say, Come and see."*
*[4] "And there went out another horse that was red:(Red stands for Communism) and power was given to him that sat thereon to take peace from the earth, and that they should kill one another: and there was given unto him __a great sword.__"*

This great sword, I believe it to be some great weapon, of modern times, now, the Lord knew, what an atomic bomb is, or an Hydrogen Bomb, is, but the people of bible times did not, so that is why I suppose, that he didn't name the weapon, just a symbol, of some great weapon, by calling it a great sword.

But In Ezekiel, he tells of sending fire on the isles, and an Isles, is a country, that was not known in that day, and my belief is that the Lord could have called the name of the United States of America, but the people of that time, wouldn't know of what he was talking of, so he just called unknown lands, Isles.

*Ezekiel 39:6 "And I will send a fire on Magog, and among them that dwell carelessly in the isles, and they shall know that I am the LORD."*

So I believe God will let man rescue Israel, to fulfill his word., for the beast, or Anti-christ will be that strong delusion, that the Lord said he would send to people who refused to believe on the Lord Jesus, and the Lord will send them that strong delusion, so that they will believe a lie, and be damned, because they will accept the beast as the Messiah.

*2ⁿᵈ Thessalonians 2:8—12—[8]* *"And then shall that wicked be revealed, whom the Lord shall consume with the spirit of his mouth, and shall destroy with the brightness of his coming."*
*[9] "Even him, whose coming is after the working of Satan with all powers and signs and lying wonders,"*
*[10] "And with all deceivableness of unrighteousness in them that perish; because they received not the love of the truth, that they might be saved."*
*[11] "And for this cause God shall send them strong delusion, that they should believe a lie:"*
*[12] "That they all might be damned who believed not the truth, but had pleasure in unrighteousness."*

I use a lot of scripture, for that is the only truth, as far as I'm concerned, now when I think that something will happen, that the scripture doesn't state, but perhaps points in that direction, then I want you to know, that is what I believe, but can't prove it exactly by God's word.

So to me that strong delusion is the anti-christ, who will rescue Israel, from that mighty army, that Russia leads, with perhaps an Hydrogen Bomb, or something in like manner now I'm not a scientist, and I don't know what all that the USA, has in it's arsenal, of weapons. Ezekiel tells us who all will be in that army, that's led by Russia, that will come against Israel, at that time and I believe this, that time will be coming soon upon this wicked world, our own country, for example, has now ruled God our of our schools, out of our public buildings, and children know next to nothing about God, and I'm afraid that God holds us, his children accountable, for that. He said,

*2ⁿᵈ Chronicles 7:14* *"my people, which are called by my name, shall humble themselves, and pray, and seek my face, and turn from their wicked ways; then will I hear from heaven, and will forgive their sin, and will heal their land."*

I know that God was speaking to Solomon, just after Solomon had finished the Temple in Jerusalem, but that verse of scripture is universal, it applies to us, his children today, just as much as it did to

Israel in Solomon's day, because he said *"IF my people"* we that are saved by God's grace, we are his people, *"Which are called by my name"*, we are called by his name, we are called Christians, which means Christ like, *"Shall humble themselves"* we are too proud, *"And Pray"*. and he's not talking about a now lay me down to sleep prayer, *"And seek my face"*, that means to ask, What would you have me to do Lord? *"And turn from their wicked ways"*, That is a strong indictment against God's people, is it not? What is wicked ways according to the Lord? The answer is not doing what the Lord has asked us to do. I don't mean to preach here, but I believe with all my heart, that is the problem with America, God's people has forgot how to do God's will.

*Ezekiel 38:1-8—[1]* *"AND the word of the LORD came unto me, saying,"*
*[2] "Son of man, set thy face against Gog, the land of Magog, the chief prince of Meshech and Tubal, and prophesy against him,"*
*[3] "And say, Thu saith the Lord GOD; Behold, I am against thee, O Gog, the chief prince of Meshech and Tubal:"*
*[4] "And I will turn thee back, and put hooks into thy jaws, and I will bring thee forth, and all thine army, horses and horsemen, all of them clothed with all sorts of armour, even a great company with bucklers and shields, all of them handling swords;"*
*[5] "Persia, Ethiopia, and Lybia with them; all of them with shields, and helmet:"*
*[6] "Gomer, and all his bands; the house of Togarmah of the north quarters, and all his bands: and many people with thee."*
*[7] "Be thou prepared, and prepare for thyself, thou, and all thy company that are assembled unto thee, and be thou a guard unto them."*
*[8] "After many days thou shalt be visited: in the latter years thou shalt come into a land that is brought back from the sword, and is gathered out of many people, against the mountains of Israel, which have been always waste: but it is brought forth out of the nations, and they shall dwell safely all of them."*

Here I think that the horses, and horsemen are symbols, of perhaps tanks and jeeps, trucks and all kinds of armament, that an army uses today, God says to the chief prince of Gog and the land of Magog, the chief prince of Meshech, and Tubal, these are the cities of Moscow, and Toblisk, the chief Prince is none other that Satan, he is the chief prince of Meshech and Tubal, and God said to Satan, I am against thee, notice, God told the prophet Ezekiel, Prophesy against HIM!

He was not talking about Latimer Putin, or the president of Russia, but against the true ruler of Russia, Satan. Back in ***Genesis 10th chapter***, it tells us where these people settled, when God changed everybody's language.

Gomer is the son of Japheth, the eldest son of Noah, and Gomer is the father of Magog, Madai, Javan, Tubal, Meshech, and Tiras, these are the ancestors of the Celtic family, from Magog descended, the predominate Russians of modern day, Madai, was the father of the Medes, Javan is the ancestor of the people of Greece, and Syria.

***Genesis 10:1-5—[1]*** *"NOW these are the generations of the sons of Noah, Shem, Ham, and Japheth: and unto them were sons born after the flood."*
*[2] "The sons of Japheth; Gomer, and Magog, and Madai, and Javan, and Tubal, and Meshech, and Tiras."*
*[3] "And the sons of Gomer; Ashkenaz, and Riphath, and Togarmah."*
*[4] "And the sons of Javan; Elishah, and Tarshish, Kittim, and Dodanim."*
*[5] "By these were the isles of the Gentiles divided in their lands; every one after his tongue, after their families, in their nations."*

These are the descendants of Japheth, the eldest of Noah, and from these are the ones, who will come against Israel in the first of the time of the Great Tribulation Period, from these came the race of the Gentiles, now there are other of the descendants of Gomer, who are not mentioned, who are not a part of this as the ones that make up that great Army. Such as Tarshish, which are the people of Spain, and Kittim, which are the People of Italy and Dodanim, are people that settled somewhere in that region. the modern day names of the makeup of that invading army, led by Russia, are, Persia, which is Iran, and surrounding states, Ethiopia, and Libya are of northern Africa, the makeup of these are the descendants of Ham, through Cush, Cush means black, and the people of Libya and Ethiopia, are dark skinned people, Now I don't want to sound raciest, in any way, for I am not, because these are all people of the descendants of Japheth, as well as the descendants of Ham, and they are attempting to destroy some of the descendants of Shem, the Israelis.

Prophesy, can't be understood, except some of History is understood, because they both, work together, to find where someone come from, works together, to find where they settled. Abraham was a descendant of Shem, but some of the descendants of Abraham, hates others of Abraham's descendants, for instance, the descendants, of Ishmael, Abraham's son by Sarah's maid, hates Israel, the descendants, of Isaac's half brother. Ishmael was not promised to Abraham, and Sarah, and Abraham, through Sarah's maid Hagar, because Sarah, thought they thought they were too old to have children, tried to help God out, and all the people of the earth, have suffered because of it.

And even other descendants of Shem, are against Israel, such as Japan, China, Korea, Vietnam, and other countries, but the reason that all these people are against Israel, is because Israel is still God's people, and most of the world is ruled by Satan, and Satan hates God, and God's children, and that is the reason of the hatred for Israel from most all nations of the world today. And the United States of America, is very swiftly turning from Israel, to our great shame, and loss of blessings, for every time the USA pressures Israel to give up land in the name of peace, America, is hit with an Earthquake, or a Hurricane, or Tornados, or great Drought, that brings great destruction, Such Storms has cost the United States in 2005 alone a total of  $56, Billion Dollars. Our Politicians are Ignorant of God's warning, "***I will Bless them that bless thee, and curse him that curseth thee***", This promise was given to Abraham, and handed down to Isaac, Jacob, and his twelve sons, The nation of Israel. I personally sent an E-mail to the White house, concerning this, at that time, but it was ignored, now they won't accept any E-mails from me. God knew that in the year of our Lord 1948, that Israel would once more be gathered out of the nations of the world, and brought back to the homeland, but it seems, that our leaders have either forgotten that fact, or just ignoring the fact, because of unbelief.

***Ezekiel 38:8—12—[8]*** *"After many days <u>thou shalt</u> be visited: in the latter years <u>thou shalt</u> come into the land that is brought back from the sword, and is gathered out of many people, against the mountains of Israel, which have been always waste: but it is brought forth out of the nations, and they shall dwell safely all of them."*

If you will notice God said twice, "***THOU SHALT***", as if he was saying, whether you want to or not, you will, come against Israel! Shalt is a word meaning, something that has to be done.

You see the Lord GOD is working things out, according to his word, and will. Speaking to Russia, and it's army, the Lord says to them———.

***Ezekiel 38:9—-12—[9]*** *"Thou shalt ascend and come like a storm, thou shalt be like a cloud to cover the land, thou, and all thy bands, and many people with thee."*
*[10] "Thus saith the Lord GOD; It shall come to pass, that at the same time shall things come into thy mind, and thou shalt think an evil thought:"*
*[11] "And <u>thou shalt</u> say, I will go up to a land of unwalled villages; I will go to them that are at rest, that dwell safely, all of them dwelling without walls, and having neither bars nor gates."*
*[12] "To take a spoil, and to take a prey; to turn thine hand upon desolate places that are now inhabited, and upon the people that are gathered out of the nations, which have gotten cattle and goods, that dwell in the midst of the land."*

If you notice again God tells them that the shalt do what he says, even if they don't want to, but Russia will decide to do things according to God's will, even though they don't believe in God. This is called God's Sovereign will.

The spoil that Russia wants, are the warm ports of The Mediterranean Sea, to ship out the oil, that they buy from Iran, and other middle east countries.

They also want the minerals that are in the Dead Sea, Worth multimillions.

Israel is a treasure trove to other nations, Iran wants it, other middle east nations, wants Israel, but if Israel were ever to be destroyed, Which it will not be, Russia would move in and take the richest little nation in the middle east.

Verse eleven, God says that Russian Army will go up, and before Russia will go down, why the difference in directions? He will come down, by way of the Atlantic Ocean, down to the Persian gulf, and Tarshish, (Spain) and Sheba, and Dedan (Saudi Arabia), will ask Russia, are you come to take great spoil?

That could mean one thing, Russia, and it's army, will most likely, come down the Atlantic coast, through the Mediterranean Sea and disembark, at Saudia Arabia, then with the Armies from there and other Muslim nations will gather with them to go up to Israel, and that is when .

***Ezekiel 38:13*** *"Sheba, and Dedan, (Saudia Arabia) and the merchants of Tarshish, (Spain), with all the young lions thereof, shall say unto thee, Art thou come to take a spoil? Hast thou gathered thy company to take a prey? To carry away silver and gold, to take away cattle and goods, to take a great spoil?"*

On in the next chapter of ***Ezekiel***, the Lord tells us that this vast army will make it to Israel, and then God will move the nation of, I believe the United States, to strike against them, and there is not much doubt, with a Hydrogen bomb, or a missile loaded with an Hydrogen war head. On Russia, and on the Russian Army that has come against Israel, and I believe one from Russia, will hit America. Now that you have the how's and the where's, let's look at the beast, and Israel, and the agreement the beast makes with Israel.

*Daniel 9:27* *"And he shall confirm the covenant with many for one week: and in the midst of the week he shall cause the sacrifice and the oblation to cease, and for the overspreading of abominations he shall make it desolate, even until the consummation, and that determined shall be poured upon the desolate."*

The beast, or anti-christ will make a covenant with Israel, and the sacrifice of lambs, and certain animals, shall be made by Israel, since Israel, has not accepted The Messiah Jesus that has come, they will once again go back to the Old Testament law and the Priesthood, and all the ordinances of the Priesthood, this is the covenant that the beast will make with Israel, for one week is the covenant, but in the middle of the week, or seven years, the beast will break that covenant and demand worship of himself instead.

*Matthew 24 :15* *"When ye therefore shall see the abomination of desolation, spoken of by Daniel the prophet, stand in the holy place, (whoso readeth, let him understand:"*

Then Jesus tells the disciples, and us, what will happen, and for Israel to flee into the mountains, that is to the mountains of Moab, Edom, and Ammon, these three countries are now found in modern day Jordan, now I'm not revealing any secrets, for Jesus did, a long time ago, back in the days of Daniel. You see the devil cannot harm the elect of Israel, and when I say the Elect, I mean the ones that God knew before the beginning of time, who would accept the true Messiah, when the time comes, and he told Moab to hide his chosen remnant of Israel.

*Matthew 24:16—22—[16]* *"Then let them which be in Judea flee into the mountains:"*
*[17]* *"Let him which is on the housetop not come down to take any thing out of his house:"*
*[18]* *"Neither let him which is in the field return back to take his clothes."*
*[19]* *"And woe unto them that are with child, and to them that give suck in those days!"*

*[20] "But pray ye that your flight be not in the winter, neither on the sabbath day:"*
*[21] "For then shall be great tribulation, such as was not since the beginning of the world to this time, no, nor ever shall be."*
*[22] "And except those days should be shortened, there should no flesh be saved: but for the elect's sake those days shall be shortened."*

Isaiah explains this to us, or at least some of it.

*Isaiah 16:4 "Let mine outcasts dwell with thee, Moab; be thou a covert to them from the face of the spoiler: for the extortioner is at an end, the spoiler ceaseth, the oppressors are consumed out of the land."*

You see, in God's foreknowledge, he knows who will trust him, and call upon him, and who will not, just as he knows if you, or I are saved, and everything about us, he knew this many eons ago, and an Eon is an undetermined amount of time.

*Daniel 12:1 "AND at that time shall Michael stand up, the great prince which standeth for the children of thy people: and there shall be a time of trouble, such as never was since there was a nation even to that same time: and at that time thy people shall be delivered, every one that shall be found written in the book."*

I have good news for all who will trust the Lord with their soul salvation, I'm speaking about the Church, none of you will have to go into the great Tribulation, period, for just before the Tribulation period begins, you will be taken out of this world, in what is known as the rapture.

Let us get back to that war, that will happen just after the calling out of the church, the Rapture of the church.

*Revelation 6:1,2—1] "AND I saw when the Lamb opened one of the seals, and I heard, as it were the noise of thunder, one of the four beasts saying, Come and see."*

*[2] "And I saw, and behold a white horse: and he that sat on him had a bow; and a crown was given unto him: and he went forth conquering, and to conquer."*

This is the little book saw in the hands of God the Father, and there was found no man able to open the little book, neither to even look upon it, they searched in heaven, and earth, and under the earth, and no man was found, who was able to open the little book, and John said, I wept much, but one of the Elders told him not to weep, and John then saw a Lamb as it had been slain, come and take this little book out of the hand of the Father.

This first seal opened, revealed the beast, or anti-christ, he was on a white horse, as if he was the Son of man, who was to come on a white horse, notice he had no arrows for his bow, meaning, he come in peace, and he will prove it, if he has to kill about everyone in the world.

This crown that will be given him, is from mankind, not God, because he will kill some of God's people, the 144,000 preachers. And he will conquer the most of the world, and two thirds of Israel. Because of the strong delusion, that God has promised he would send to all unbelievers, when the Rapture happens.

*Zechariah 13:8,9—[8] "And it shall come to pass, that in all the land, (Israel) saith the LORD, two parts therein shall be cut off and die; but the third shall be left therein."*
*[9] "And I will bring the third part through the fire (Tribulation period) and will refine them as silver is refined, and will try them as gold is tried:" they shall call on my name, and I will say, It is my people: and they shall say, the LORD is my God."*

Two thirds of the nation of Israel will accept the mark of the beast, and will be cut off from God, and his blessings, but one third of the nation of Israel, will call on the Lord, and the Lord will be pleased with them, and he will say, ***It is my people.***"

Back to the war, of Ezekiel, and the damage it does to the people of the earth.

*Revelation 6:5,6—[5] "And when he had opened the third seal, I heard the third beast say, Come and see. And I beheld, and lo, a black horse: and he that sat on him had a pair of balances in his hand."*
*[6] "And I heard a voice in the midst of the four beasts say, A measure of wheat for a penny, and three measures of barley for a penny; and see that thou hurt not the oil and the wine."*

This is a direct result of a nuclear war, a great famine, shortage of food for mankind, and when the Lamb of God opens the next seal, we find more carnage, more destruction, and death.

# CHAPTER SEVEN

## *THE FOURTH SEAL!*

*Revelation 6:7,8—[7] "And when he had opened the fourth seal, I heard the voice of the fourth beast say, Come and see."*
*[8] "And I looked, and behold a pale horse: and his name that sat on him was Death, and Hell followed after him. And power was given unto them over the fourth part of the earth, to kill with the sword, and with hunger, and with death, and with the beasts of the earth."*

Not only will there be a famine of food for mankind, but there will be a shortage of food for the animal kingdom, and it says that the beasts of the earth will kill mankind, for food.

This is just a part of what the lost people will have to put up with, and suffer greatly during the Tribulation period, but then after the Great White Throne Judgment, and then be cast into the lake of fire where the beast, and the false prophet, and the devil will be for all eternity.

All this will be caused by this Russian invasion into Israel, where only one sixth of this invading army will be allowed to return home, now this has to happen to fulfill all of God's prophesy, because after the Reign of Christ on this earth for one thousand years, there will also be another Russian uprising, and Russia headed up by Satan, will attempt a one last ditch effort to defeat the Lord, but God will rain down on Russia, and all it's allies fire and brimstone from heaven, and wipe out all wickedness on this earth.

Now back to ***Ezekiel 39———————————-.***

***Ezekiel 39: 1-6—[1] "THEREFORE, thou son of man prophesy against Gog, and say, Thus saith the Lord GOD; Behold, I am against thee, O Gog, the chief prince of Meshech and Tubal:"***

Remember the chief prince of Meshech and Tubal, or Moscow, and Tobolsk, and the next verse tells us this is not the battle of Armageddon, for at Armageddon, the entire army, there will be destroyed by the Lord Jesus, but here in Ezekiel 39, one sixth of this invading army will be allowed to go home, to have more children, so that at the end of the Reign of Christ for one thousand years, will have a great army to once again come against Israel. where all wickedness shall be purged from the earth.

***Ezekiel 39"2-6—[2] "And I will turn thee back, and leave but the sixth part of thee, and will cause thee to come up from the north parts, and will bring thee upon the mountains of Israel:"***

The one sixth part of this invading army will be allowed to return home, and the rest of this verse speaks of the entire army coming up from the north parts, Russia, upon the mountains of Israel, where they will be wiped out, all but a sixth part.

***[3] "And I will smite thy bow out of thy left hand, and will cause thine arrows to fall out of thy right hand,"***

What but a bomb of some kind could do this to this Russian led army? Now I know God could with a word do it, but by winning this war, the beast will gain power over the entire world.

***[4] "Thou shalt fall upon the mountains of Israel, thou, and all thy bands, and the people that is with thee: I will give thee unto the ravenous birds of every sort, and to the beasts of the field to be devoured."***
***[5] "Thou shalt fall upon the open field: for I have spoken it, saith the Lord GOD."***

47

If you will notice, the word S-H-A-L-T, it is a word signifying, something that has to be done, there is no other way.

The reason here to use the term, "The Lord GOD, is that there are three that bear witness in heaven, the Father, the Word, and the Holy Ghost" as revealed to us in *1st John 5:7.,* and if you will notice in the Old Testament, it is mostly, The LORD God", see the difference, here it is referring to Jesus Christ, the Word of God, but here in these verses, he uses the term of the God -head, in complete agreement. Is addressed as The Father, The Word, The Holy Ghost.

**[6] "And I will send a fire on Magog, and among them that dwell carelessly in the isles: and they shall know that I am the LORD."**

This will take you back to *Revelation 6,* where the pale horse brings death by Radiation, poisoning. At least that sounds like what it describes, to me, and the natural food, for the animals, seems to have been destroyed. The following is said about the beast, or anti-christ, when he wins this war, because they will think that only God could win this war, now God will cause the beast to win this war, but to the people of the world, it could be only as God calls him, the beast.

*Revelation 13:4 "And they worshipped the dragon which gave power unto the beast: and they worshipped the beast, saying, Who is like unto the beast? Who is able to make war with him?"*

And they worshiped the beast, and said who is like unto the beast? So apparently to the people of the earth at this time, he will be the supposed Messiah, that Israel is still waiting for, even at this time, but the 144,000, will not receive him, but preach against him, and that is why they will be killed, because he wants to be a god, and pronounce that he is God, and two thirds of Israel will accept him as the promised Messiah, they have been looking for. Also, the majority of the world will exalt him to be a god, and in the middle of the Tribulation period, he will break his covenant with Israel, and move into the temple and demand that people worship him. [The reason that I write this, is because it is all connected, God has allowed him to rescue Israel, when there seemed to be no hope for Israel, but all of it is to fulfill God's word, while reducing the population of the world, of those who will never, and has never trusted the Lord Jesus Christ, to be the Saviour.

Remember the scripture, found in the book of ***John chapter 3: verse 36.***

***John 3:36*** *"He that believeth on the Son hath everlasting life: and he that believeth not the Son shall not see life; but **the wrath of God abideth on him.**"*

People that refuse to believe on the Son of God, has the wrath of God, on them, and WRATH is anger with a vengeance, and God will avenge himself of those who refuse to believe, "BELIEVETH" meant complete Trust, in the 1600'S when the word of God was translated into the English of that day . So that's how anyone get's saved, is by completely trusting the Lord with their soul.

***Romans 10:9*** *"That if thou shalt confess with thy mouth the Lord Jesus, and shalt believe in thine heart that God hath raised him from the dead, thou shalt be saved."*

And again, the word S-H-A-L-T, means something that has to be done, there is no other way. The covenant that the beast will make with Israel, is that they can have the temple in Jerusalem, and sacrifice animals as they did in Old Testament times, for the orthodox Jew has never accepted the true Messiah, the Lord Jesus Christ. In the sixth chapter of Isaiah, where the Lord told Isaiah to shut their eyes, so they can't see, and stop up their ears, so they couldn't hear, make their hearts fat, so they can't understand, and you might ask why all that? Well the only answer that I can find, is so many times Israel turned there backs on the Lord, and began to worship other so called gods, and also, it was so that the church could be introduced to the world, through Jesus the Christ.

***Isaiah 6:9,10—[9]*** *"And he said, Go, and tell this people, (Israel) hear ye indeed, but understand not; and see ye indeed, but perceive not."*

*[10] "Make the heart fat, and make their ears heavy, and shut their eyes; lest they see with their eyes, and hear with their ears, and understand with their heart, and convert, and be healed."*

Now the Lord didn't just come up with this idea, or notion, just for kicks, he knew in his fore knowledge, that those who refused to believe, would never believe in the Lord Jesus Christ, and since they were hell bound, because of their refusal to believe, when the Son of God came and told them he was the Son of God, they would crucify him on the cross, thinking they were doing God a favor, they were fulfilling his word.

And when Isaiah asked the Lord., how long would Israel be in this fix, God answered him, in **verses 11,12,13.**

**Isaiah 6:11** *"Then said I, Lord, how long? And he answered, until the cities be wasted without inhabitant, and the houses without man, and the land be utterly desolate,"*

This happened long ago, when Israel was dispersed, all over the world, and after world war two, Israel once again became a nation, but Israel was once again, betrayed, when Great Brittan, gave the best land to the Arabs, and the worst to Israel, in 1948. And in **Isaiah 6:12**, the Lord answers Isaiah, further, and said the following.

**Isaiah 6:12** *"And the LORD have removed men far away, and there be a great forsaking in the midst of the land."*

"And the Lord have removed men far away", meaning the Rapture of the church, then there, would be a great forsaking, in the midst of the land, meaning that two thirds of Israel, will accept the mark of the beast during the last half of the Time of the Great Tribulation period, then would the Lord return to Israel, and redeem a Remnant, out of Israel, and Egypt, as well as Assyria.

**Zechariah 13:8,9—[8]** *"And it shall come to pass, that in all the land, saith the LORD, two parts therein shall be cut off and die; but the third shall be left therein."*
*[9] "And I will bring the third part through the fire, and will refine them as silver is refined, and will try them as gold is tried:*

*they shall call on my name, and I will hear them: I will say, It is my people: and they shall say, The LORD is my God."*

Then we go back to *Isaiah 6th Chapter.*, telling of the firstfruits of Israel, the tenth of the harvest.

*Isaiah 6:13 "But yet in it shall be a tenth, and it shall return, and shall be eaten: as a teil tree, and as an oak, whose substance is in them, when they cast their leaves: so the holy seed shall be the substance thereof."*

Here God speaks of the Tithe that Israel owes the Lord, the firstfruits, for the tenth, of the total harvest, the 144,000, preachers, shall be eaten up by the world, killed by the beast, whose substance in them, is the seed of God, the Lord Jesus Christ.

*Revelation 14:1-5—[1] "AND I looked, and lo, a Lamb stood on the mount Sion, and with him an hundred forty and four thousand, having his Father's name written in their foreheads."*
*[2] "And I heard a voice from heaven as the voice of a great thunder: and I heard the voice of harpers harping with their harps:"*
*[3] "And they sung as it were a new song before the throne, and before the four beasts, and the elders: and no man could learn that song but the hundred and forty and four thousand, which were redeemed from the earth."*
*[4] "These are they which were not defiled with women; for they are virgins. These are they which follow the Lamb whithersoever he goeth. These were redeemed from among men, being the firstfruits unto God and to the Lamb."*
*[5] "And in their mouth was found no guile: for they are without fault before the throne of God."*

If you will notice, in verse four, they are called the **"FIRSTFRUITS"** which in the Old Testament, a tithe is called the firstfruits, the first tenth of every harvest, so the 144,000, Israelis, are the tithe to God from Israel, and they are the Firstfruits, of the complete harvest of souls of the Israelis, to the Lord.

*Exodus 34:22,26—[22]* *"And thou shalt observe the feast of weeks, of the first fruits of wheat harvest, and the feast of ingathering at the year's end."*
*[26]* *"The first of the firstfruits of thy land thou shalt bring unto the house of the LORD thy God. Thou shalt not seethe a kid in his mother's milk."*

The firstfruits is the tithe, the tenth of the harvest, so will the 144,000, be the tithe to God. One tenth of the complete harvest. I repeat this about the first tenth, because it is very important to remember, and to understand, for this is the number of Israelis that will be saved during the seven years of the great Tribulation Period, Multiply 144,000, X 10= 1,440,000 Israelis that will be saved at that time, and then go to *Isaiah 19: 22—25,* and you will find the total of persons that will be saved during that same time, of seven years.

*Isaiah 19:22—25—[22]* *"And the LORD shall smite Egypt: he shall smite and heal it: and they shall return even to the LORD, and he shall be intreated of them, and shall heal them."*
*[23]* *"In that day shall there be a highway out of Egypt to Assyria. And the Assyrian shall come into Egypt, and the Egyptians shall serve with the Assyrians."*
*[24]* *"In that day shall Israel be the third with Egypt and with Assyria, even a blessing in the midst of the land:"*
*[25]* *"Whom the LORD of hosts shall bless, saying, Blessed be Egypt my people, and Assyria the work of my hands, and Israel mine inheritance."*

This tells us how many people will be saved during the seven years of Great Tribulation, *1,440,000 Israelis*, *1,440,000, Egyptians*, *1,440,000 Assyrians*, add them up, and you come up with,— *4,320,000, people* that will be saved during that time. But you might say, I thought that there would be a multitude saved that no man could number, at that time, NO, there will not be, for *Revelation 7:9,* is misunderstood, by many Preachers and Teachers, for I myself have heard this since I was saved by God's grace, and let's look at that verse of scripture.

The reason that I use some words in blue, instead of the

traditional black, is because I want to put them into close attention, to the readers.

***Revelation 7:9*** *"After this I beheld, and, lo, a great multitude, which no man could number, of all nations, and kindreds, and people, and tongues, stood before the throne, and before the Lamb, clothed with white robes, and palms in their hands;"*

This could be only the Old Testament Saints, and the Church age Saints, for they have on their white robes, and the church only could come from every nation, every tongue, every kindred, during the time that John was seeing the seven years of Tribulation, these were already in heaven, praising God, and the Lamb. The church had already been before the Judgement Seat of Christ, and been rewarded, But you might say that in ***Revelation 7:14,*** that they came out of great tribulation, yes it does say that, but the Old Testament Saints, and the Church age Saints, have been in great tribulation, every since, Adam and Eve, were put out of the garden of Eden. If you don't accept that, then if you are saved, look back on your own life, and know that you have had a lot of trouble, since you got saved by God's grace, and trying to live right in the sight of the Lord. Some places I will repeat myself, just to show, the truth, and by repeating it, it get's in your brain, more swiftly. Also that is why I have used the same verses of scripture, to keep in your mind, what God is doing, and what happens to the remnant of Israel.

When Daniel was praying and confessing his sins, and the sins of his people, he was petitioning the Lord as to what was going to happen to the people of Israel, because it did seem that God was angry with Israel, and the Prophet Daniel, was worried concerning the nation of Israel, and the Lord started to explain, through the Angel Gabriel.

***Daniel 9:24-27—[24]*** *"Seventy weeks are determined upon thy people and upon thy holy city, to finish the transgression, and to make an end of sins, and to make reconciliation for iniquity, and to bring in everlasting righteousness, and to seal up the vision and prophesy, and to anoint the most Holy."*

Let me stop here and explain, by the help of the Lord, what is to take place for the house of Israel, Gabriel is explaining to Daniel what will take place with the people of Israel, and to encourage the prophet, as to what was going to take place with Daniel's people Israel.

Seventy weeks of years was going to happen with Israel, and these seventy weeks began with the decree of Cyrus the Persian, when he sent back to Israel, Ezra, and Nehemiah, back to Israel to restore the walls of the city of Jerusalem, and to rebuild the Temple in Jerusalem, that was destroyed by Nebbuchadnezzar, and his army, and the return of the children of Israel, and continues to on to the time of the Lord's second stage of his second coming, when he comes from the East, bring the remnant of Israel, that God has hid from the face of the Anti-christ, the last half of the Seven Year Great Tribulation Period. In the mountains of modern day Jordan.

**_Daniel 9:25_ _"Know therefore and understand, that from the going forth of the commandment to restore and to build Jerusalem unto the Messiah the prince shall be seven weeks, and threescore and two weeks: the street shall be built again, and the wall, even in troublous times."_**

This continues the Narrative of Gabriel, to Daniel, explaining to Daniel, concerning, his people Israel, from the commandment of Cyrus the king of Persia, for Nehemiah, to rebuild the wall of Jerusalem, to the Birth of the Lord Jesus would be seven weeks, and threescore and two weeks, as well as the street of Jerusalem, and in troubling times, because the people that lived around Jerusalem, made lot's of trouble for Nehemiah and the ones with him, in the attempt to stop the rebuilding of the walls of Jerusalem.

Seven weeks plus threescore and two weeks amount to 434 years. From the commandment of Cyrus, till the birth of the Messiah, Jesus Christ, the only begotten Son of God.

**_Daniel 9: 26_ _"And after threescore and two weeks shall Messiah be cut off, but not for himself: and the people of the prince that shall come shall destroy the city and the sanctuary: and the end thereof shall be with a flood, and unto the end of the war desolations are determined."_**

After 434 years, the Messiah shall be cut off, but not for himself, this was the crucifixion, of the Lord Jesus, but he will not die for himself, but will die for the people of the whole world, and the prince that will come is Titus the Roman Emperor, who destroys the temple, and the city of Jerusalem, and destroys the walls of the city. **_A.D. 70._**

**_Daniel 9:27_** *"And he shall confirm the covenant with many for one week: (Anti-christ) and in the midst of the week he shall cause the sacrifice and the oblation to cease, and for the overspreading of abominations he shall make it desolate, even until the consummation, and that determined shall be poured upon the desolate."*

At the middle of three and one half years, the Anti-christ declares himself to be god, and he demands worship, from the people of the world, since the majority of the world believes him to be the Messiah, he begins to believe it himself.

**_Daniel 9:44,45—[44]_** *"But tidings out of the east and out of the north shall trouble him: therefore he shall go forth with great fury to destroy, and utterly to make away many."*

The Anti-christ will hear of things in the East, which is east of Jerusalem, which is Syria, Iran, most all of the Arab nations, and he will hear of things going on in the North, which is Russia, Germany, France, England, Ireland, and all the Celtic nations, the descendants of Gomer, and the anti-christ will hear of the plans to attack Israel, and he shall go forth with great fury to destroy, and to utterly make away many.

**_Daniel 9:45_** *"And he shall plant the tabernacles of his Palace between the seas in the glorious holy mountain (Jerusalem) yet he shall come to his end, and none shall help him."* (beast)

He shall move to Jerusalem, and set up his headquarters there, after he rescues Israel, and declare that he is god, and demand that people worship him, yet he shall come to his end, and none shall help him, and that speaks of when the Lord comes on a white horse, and fights the battle of Armageddon, and throws the anti-christ, and the false prophet into the lake of fire and brimstone. I honestly believe that God will hold on to the USA, and the President of the USA, at that time, will be the anti-christ, for the USA has all the weapons, it will take to wipe out most of this great army that comes against Israel, such as the Hydrogen Bomb, which kills all life for a certain area around the attack zone, but will not hurt, or destroy Tanks, guns, Air Planes, or any kind of weapons, or buildings.

But human life will be eliminated, for a great area, of this part of the world.

Now I have given to you, the **_When_**, and the **_Where_**, also the **_Why,_** this all takes place, remember this, God is always in Charge, of the things of this world, and when all of this is over, God will still be in charge. Also if you will study God's word as his word commands his children to, then you can find this all in the KJV, the **_Authorized King James Version of the Bible_**.

The result of the attack on Israel, by Magog, or Russia, and all his bands, and no all the armies of the world cannot defeat the Word of God, what he says he will do, you can be sure, he will do it.

**_Ezekiel 39:1—6—[1]_** *"THEREFORE, thou son of man, prophesy against Gog, and say, Thus the Lord GOD; Behold, I am against thee, O Gog, the chief prince of Meshech and Tubal:" (_Moscow & Tobolsk_)*

*[2] "And I will turn thee back, and leave but the sixth part of thee, (1/6) and will cause thee to come up from the north parts, and will bring thee upon the mountains of Israel."*

*[3] "And I will smite thy bow out of thy left hand, and will cause thine arrows to fall out of thy right hand."*

*[4] "Thou shalt fall upon the mountains of Israel, thou, and all thy bands, and the people that is with thee: I will give thee unto the ravenous birds of every sort, and to the beasts of the field to be devoured."*

*[5] "Thou shalt fall upon the open field: for I have spoken it, saith the Lord GOD."*

*[6] And I will send a fire on Magog, and among them, that dwell carelessly in the isles; and they shall know I Am the LORD."*

These weapons mentioned here, are weapons of Ezekiel's time, God knew about the Nuclear power of Russia, and it's allies, but the prophet did not, so he used weapons that Ezekiel would know and understand, and when he uses the word S-H-A-L-T, he speaks of something that has to be done, that is what SHALT means, Something that has to be done, so as God prophesied, it is exactly what he will do. Also you will find other Words will **_signify_** something special, and they are these two words, Lord GOD, when most of the time it is used the LORD God, notice the reversal, when it is presented the Lord GOD, it means, in verse one, Almighty God, Or El-Shaddai, the satisfying one, and makes one fruitful, whereas, the term LORD God, means **_Jehovah Elohim._**

Many people mis-interpret **_Revelation 13:1-3,_** as to think that an Emperor has revived from the dead, or some even think the beast could be Ronald Wilson Raegan, because his name equals to 666, six letters in each of his names, but that is incorrect, as well, it is not someone who was dead, and revived, because a person who is dead, if he, or she could come back to this earth, if their soul was in hell, they would come back preaching against sin, not doing something to provoke, the wrath of God, and if that soul was in heaven, you could never get him, or her to come back to this wicked earth, without them preaching God's word, and warning people on earth, of the dangers, and torments of hell, and preaching how sweet heaven is.

**_Revelation 13:1-3—[1]_** *"AND I stood upon the sand of the sea, and saw a beast rise up out of the sea, having seven heads and ten horns, and upon his horns ten crowns, and upon his heads the name of blasphemy."*
*[2] "And the beast which I saw was like a leopard, and his feet were as the feet of a bear, and his mouth as the mouth of a lion: and the dragon gave him his power, and his seat, and great authority."*
*[3] "And I saw one of his heads as it were wounded to death; and his deadly wound was healed: and all the world wondered after the beast."*

First of all let me explain about the two legs of the Image, that Daniel saw, in—————,

*Daniel 2:31—33—[31]* *"Thou, O king, sawest, and behold a great image. This great image, whose brightness was excellent stood before thee; and the form thereof was terrible."*
*[32]* *"This image's head was of fine gold, his breast and his arms of silver, his belly and his thighs of brass."*
*[33]* *"His legs of iron, his feet part of iron and part clay."*

Each part of this image represented each of the great kingdoms of the world, the head represented the Babylon kingdom, the head of gold, and then the breast and it's arms represented the Medes and the Persian kingdom, of silver, and notice each kingdom became worth less and less, the belly and it's thighs were of brass, represented the kingdom of Greece, under Alexander the great, then it's two legs, represent the old Roman Empire, that was divided, Eastern and Western Empire, one headquarters was in Rome, and another headquarters was in Turkey, Istanbul, Turkey, and it is said that Constantine, the Roman Emperor was headed to Istanbul, Turkey to kill the Emperor of the Roman Empire of Istanbul, Turkey, and on his way there, he was supposed to have seen a sign in the sky that gave him the sign of Victory, and he in turn, had each of his soldiers to paint a cross on each Shield, which was the ancient sign of Ank, not the cross of Jesus Christ, and he had each of his soldiers baptized, and then went on to Istanbul, and won the victory, and destroyed the eastern part of the Empire. Afterwards returning to Rome, Italy, he began to see this empire dissolving, and that was when, he changed his Emperor Robes, to a Religious Robe, the Robe of the first Pope, dissolving the Roman Empire. And this is the head, that will be restored during the reign of the Beast, the Old Roman Empire will be restored under the Leadership of the Beast, because every Roman Emperor, was to be worshiped, as a god, after their death. This was when the Catholic church began under the first Pope Constantine. Approximately *314 A.D.* And the worship of the Roman Pope will be reinstated, in the Beast. And it was the Old Roman Empire that became dead, and will be revived, under the Beast, or Anti-christ. Not a man, but an Empire. This was when the Roman Catholic church began to gain ground,—,

***Revelation 2: 6*** *"But this thou hast, that thou hatest the deeds of the Nicolaitanes, which I also hate."*

The Nicolaitanes, were a priestly order that sprang up under the leadership of Constantine, the first Pope.

The name of Nicolaitanes, was taken from Niko, which means to conquer, and Laos, means the people, or Laity, and what was beginning in the church of Ephesus, was growing, and finally in Pergamos, became a doctrine,——,

***Revelation 2:15*** *"So hast thou also them that hold the doctrine of the Nicolaitanes, which thing I hate."*

This happened approximately ***316 AD***. The third century after the Death, burial, and resurrection of our Lord Jesus Christ.

# CHAPTER EIGHT

# Old Roman Empire Revived

A warning is found of such lordship over God's flock in————,

*1ˢᵗ Peter 5:2,3—[2] "Feed the flock of God which is among you, taking the oversight thereof, not by constraint, but willingly; not for filthy lucre, but of a ready mind."*
*[3] "Neither as being lords over God's heritage, but being ensamples to the flock."*

In other words the Pastors are to feed God's flock, not by oversight, or by Constraint, but willingly, not for money, but in readiness, to preach the gospel of the Lord Jesus Christ. Not being lords over the flock, but serving as examples before the flock, which God has placed them over. But The Message is, That it is the OLD ROMAN EMPIRE that is Revived. Not a man, but an Empire under the leadership of the anti-christ, or beast.

Every Christian should get a copy of the book, *The Two Babylons, by Alexander Hyslop*. And study it along with God's word, and could learn quite a bit of information, from both the Authorized King James Bible, and the book "*The Two Babylons*" *by Alexander Hyslop.*

The beast will be put in power when he wins this war to rescue Israel, helped along by the great whore, spoken of in *Revelation 17ᵗʰ chapter.*

*Revelation 17:1-7—[1] "AND there came one of the seven angels which had the seven vials, and talked with me, saying unto me, Come hither; I will shew unto thee the judgement of the great whore that sitteth upon many waters:"*
*[2] "With whom the kings of the earth have committed fornication, and the inhabitants of the earth have been made drunk with the wine of her fornication."*
*[3] "So he carried me away in the spirit into the wilderness: and I saw a woman sit upon a scarlet coloured beast, full of names of blasphemy, having seven heads and ten horns."*
*[4] "And the woman was arrayed in purple and scarlet colour, and decked with gold and precious stones and pearls, having a golden cup in her hand full of abominations and filthiness of her fornication:"*
*[5] "And upon her forehead was a name written MYSTERY, BABYLON THE GREAT, THE MOTHER OF HARLOTS AND ABOMINATIONS OF THE EARTH."*
*[6] "And I saw the woman drunken with the blood of the saints, and with the blood of the martyrs of Jesus: and when I saw her, I wondered with great admiration."*
*[7] "And the angel said unto me, Wherefore didst thou marvel? I will tell thee the mystery of the woman, and of the beast that carrieth her, which hath the seven heads and ten horns."*

Always in scripture, a church is mention in the female gender, and this is the same so-called church, that started back in **Revelation 2:6,** and grew until this time, carried on by the church of Pergamos, also in chapter two of Revelation, approximately 316 AD. And it grew even until, this time of the Great Tribulation, of seven years, and God's word even tells us where the headquarters of the great whore is found .

*Revelation 17:8—12—[8] "The beast that thou sawest was, and is not; and shall ascend out of the bottomless pit, and go into perdition: and they that dwell on the earth shall wonder, whose names were not written in the book of life from the foundation of the world, when they behold the beast that was, and is not, and yet is."*

I would like to stop here and explain, some of the wording found here in this verse of scripture. The beast that thou sawest was, and is not, is a man, most likely an handsome man, with a lot of Charisma, yet without conscience, he has a beastly nature, he is not actually a beast, like a lion, or bear, but a human being, without a conscience, toward God. And when he wins this war, and rescues Israel from Russian led army, that sets out to do away with Israel, whom the devil hates, and most of the world, simply because Israel is God's people. And the people will say about him.

*Revelation 13:4* *"And they worshipped the beast, saying, Who is like unto the beast? Who is able to make war with him."*

This will soon go to his head, as the saying goes, and then he will begin to believe his own lies.

*Revelation 17:9* *"And here is the mind which hath wisdom. The seven heads are seven mountains, on which the woman sitteth."*

None other than the seven hills of Rome, on which sits the Vatican, it is the Catholic church, this is the great whore, that God's word describes.

*Revelation 17:10* *"And there are seven kings: five are fallen, and one is, and the other is not yet come; and when he cometh, he must continue a short space."*

The seven kings are as follows, *[1] Julius Ceasar* he was assassinated, *[2] -Tiberius*—He was poisoned. [3] *Caligula*- He was assassinated. [4] *Claudous*-He was poisoned. [5] *Nero-* He commited suicide. [6] *Domation*- the one that is, that was Emperor that exiled the apostle John on the isle of Patmos, after John won his wife and son to the Lord Jesus Christ. [7] He was *Constantine*, the last Emperor, the one that changed his Emperor Robes, for the Religious Robes of the first Pope. [8] will be the *anti-christ, or the beast.*

These names were not all the Emperors of Rome, but these seven are the ones, that God, speaks of in his word.

***Revelation 17: 11*** *"And the beast that was, and is not, even he is the eighth, and is of the seven, and goeth into perdition."*

It states in ***verse 8, of Revelation 17***, that the beast comes out of, or ascends out of the bottomless pit, because he is completely sold out to Satan, and will go into perdition, for the same reason. Having a beastly nature.

***Revelation 17: 12*** *"And the ten horns which thou sawest are ten kings, which have received no kingdom as yet; but receive power as kings one hour with the beast."*

These ten kings will receive power with the beast, just for the seemingly importance of being a king, also sold out to Satan. There is a gap if you will between ***verse 13-15***, which speaks of the church, and the other saints, Israel, Egypt, and Assyria, that will be with the Lord at Armageddon, then chapter seventeen goes back to the time during the great tribulation, and these ten kings will hate the whore, and give their power to the beast, to destroy the great whore.

***Revelation 17:16-18—[16]*** *"And the ten horns which thou sawest upon the beast, these shall hate the whore, and shall make her desolate and naked, and shall eat her flesh, and burn her with fire."*

These ten kings, that the beast will pick out to be kings, will be those, who, will bend to his every whim, and give themselves over to him completely, as his puppets, with the pull of the string, it would seem so.

***Revelation 17:17*** *"For God hath put in their hearts to fulfil his will, and to agree, and give their kingdom unto the beast, until the words of God shall be fulfilled."*

For God will put into their hearts, to hate the whore, and to give their kingdoms to the beast, to destroy the great whore, now I've not said much, about the false prophet, but he will be a Pope. And his job is to put the beast into power, or help the beast to gain power over all the world, and he is the second beast we find in ***Revelation 13——.***

***Revelation 13:11*** *"And I beheld another beast coming up out of the earth; and he had two horns like a lamb, and he spake as a dragon."*

This is none other than the false prophet, that helps to put into power the beast, by advertising the beast as the Messiah, that has come to the earth, to help Israel, and he is part of the deception, to turn the beast into the strong delusion, that God said he would send to all who refuses to believe in the Lord Jesus Christ, the false prophet would have to be a strong religious man, with a lot of influence, and who better than the Pope.

***Revelation 13:12*** *"And he exerciseth all the power of the first beast before him, and causeth the earth and them which dwell therein to worship the first beast, whose deadly wound was healed."*

The false prophet is im-powered by the same source, the devil, Satan, the great red dragon, and it is said, that he exercises the same power as the beast, and it is he, that causes the world to take the mark either in their right hand, or their forehead. The statement, ***"Whose deadly wound was healed"***,

Could only be the organization, that he resurrected, the old Roman Empire, whose deadly wound that will be healed, it was the first Pope that killed the organization, and the same religious order to resurrect it.

***Revelation 13:13*** *"And he doeth great wonders, so that he maketh fire come down from heaven on the earth in the sight of men."*

This was what Malachi Prophesied that would happen ———.

***Malachi 4:5,6———[5]*** *"Behold, I will send you Elijah the prophet before the coming of the great and dreadful day of the LORD:"* *[6] "And he shall turn the heart of the fathers to the children, and the heart of the children to their fathers, lest I come and smite the earth with a curse."*

And in ***Revelation 13:13,*** it states that God would send Elijah the prophet back here to the earth, and knowing that the Israelites, would know the scriptures concerning them, they would believe this man, and two thirds of Israel will believe, that he is Elijah, and take the mark. For he is able to call fire down from heaven, or from some kind of Satellite, for he would have the power to do such a feat, and since God knows who will take the mark of the beast, he let's it happen.

***Revelation 13:14*** *"And deceiveth them that dwell on the earth by the means of those miracles which he had power to do in the sight of the beast; saying to them that dwell on the earth, that they should make an image to the beast, which had the wound by the sword, and did live."*

Here it states that the beast had a wound by the sword and did live, it was most likely a superficial wound, but advertised as a deadly wound, this wound seems to be different from the first deadly wound, now I'm guessing on this, but I know that if a person was dead, he either went to heaven, or to hell, and either place, if he came back from either place, it is something, he would either preach hell so hot, that people would not want to go there, and would repent, or if he was in heaven and came back, he would never do anything that would cause him to be cast into the lake of fire and brimstone, for any person, that goes to heaven, becomes like God, knowing all things, for he would be an heir, and a joint heir with Christ, as stated in———————————————.

***Romans 8:17*** *"And if children, then heirs; heirs of God, and joint- heirs with Christ; if so be that we suffer with him, that we may be also glorified with him."*

And if he was in hell, he would be like the rich man, that went to hell, he would want to win others to the Lord, and not to ruin them, and cause them to go to the lake of fire and brimstone.

***Revelation 13: 15*** *"And he had power to give life unto the image of the beast, that the image of the beast should both speak, and cause that as many as would not worship the image of the beast should be killed."*

Satan at this time seemed to have almost, anything he wanted, but it is always God who is in charge, even at this time in this world. Maybe, he doesn't know it, but he is just fulfilling God's word.

***Revelation 13:16,17—[16]*** *"And he causeth all, both small and great, rich and poor, free and bond, to receive a mark in their right hand, or in their foreheads:"*
*[17]* *"And that no man might buy or sell, save he that had the mark, or the name of the beast, or the number of his name."*

The number is 666, or the name of the beast, whoever he will be. Only God knows at this time. The time of the Great Tribulation period of seven years, and especially the last three and one half years, will be a troublesome time, and the children of Israel will be the center point of all the trouble, it is a time, when God lets the Beast divide Israel, not the land of Israel, but the people of Israel, for two thirds of Israel will accept the Beast as being their Messiah, but one third of Israel will not accept him, as being the Messiah, thus, the beast divides the nation of Israel.

God has said he would send fire on Russia, and the Isles (unknown countries at that time in history) . ***Ezekiel 39:6*** *"And I will send a fire on Magog, and them that dwell carelessly in the isles: and they shall know that I am the LORD."*

God said he would send fire on Russia, and the other countries that dwell carelessly, or that have been careless how they have treated Israel, God's people But the apostle Paul, writes something that might be hard to understand, to some, who doesn't study God's word as they should, and it was hard for me to understand this, until, later, finally I understood, the meaning of his writings, in,

***Romans 9: 6,7—[6]*** *"Not as though the word of God hath taken none effect. For they are not all Israel, which are of Israel:"*
*[7]* *"Neither, because they are the seed of Abraham, are they all children: but, In Isaac shall thy seed be called."*

First of all, the name Israel, is known as the Prince with God, and not all Israel, will be a prince with God, at the time of the beast, but those who refuse the beast, will be, A prince with God."

*John 5:40-43—[40] "And ye will not come to me, that ye might have life."*
*[41] "I receive not honour from men."*
*[42] "But I know you, that ye have not the love of God in you."*
*[43] "I am come in my Father's name, and ye receive me not; if another shall come in his own name, him ye will receive."*

Jesus Prophesied of the coming of the anti-christ, or the beast, in these verses of scripture, and since he is God, as much as the Father is God, he will bring to pass every word, that he has prophesied, would happen, thus the Beast, will divide the power of his people Israel, because two thirds of Israel will accept the beast as being the Messiah, but one third will refuse to accept the beast as being the promised Messiah. God has spoken, what will be, and none of us is able to change, one word of prophesy, our duty is to understand it, and act accordingly, and it is the duty of all saved by grace individuals, to warn others, as to what will take place, in the future, but you might say, that you don't understand a lot of the scripture, and that is the trouble with a lot of God's people, because most do not obey God's command, to study the word of God, and yes it is a command. Just as it is commanded, that we do not steal, we are commanded to study God's word.

*2nd Timothy 2:15—19—[15] "Study to shew thyself approved unto God, a workman the needeth not to be ashamed, rightly dividing the word of truth."*
*[16] "But shun profane and vain babblings: for they will increase unto more ungodliness."*
*[17] "And their word will eat as doth a canker: of whom is Hymenaeus and Philetus:"*
*[18] "Who concerning the truth have erred, saying that the resurrection is past already; and overthrow the faith of some."*
*[19] "Nevertheless the foundation of God standeth sure, having this seal, The Lord knoweth them that are his. And, Let every one that nameth the name of Christ depart from iniquity."*

The word "Profane", means Debasing what is sacred, Irreverent, Blasphemous, and "Vain babblings," means to utter indistinct, meaningless sounds or to talk idly or foolishly, or cause confusion. For the word of Hymenaeus and Philetus, was causing confusion, among a lot of God's people, by saying the resurrection, was past already, and over throw's the faith of some, causing confusion, among God's people. With a population of 1.2 billion people, India is the world's largest democracy and has upgraded it's relationship with Israel significantly, in the last two decades since renewing diplomatic relations in 1992, India and Israel have joined in counter-terrorism efforts, and have increased trade and economic ties, and Israeli high tech companies and start-up companies are increasingly outsourcing much of their development to India. In agriculture, cooperation which encompasses water management, dairy farming, horticulture and floriculture.

And one thing sure, is God promised to Abraham, passed down to Isaac, to Jacob, and all Israel ***Genesis 12:3*** *"And I will bless them that bless thee, and curse him that curseth thee: and in thee shall all families of the earth be blessed."*

***Zechariah 12:3*** *"And in that day will I make Jerusalem a burdensome stone for all people: all that burden themselves with it shall be cut in pieces, though all people of the earth be gathered against it."*

# CHAPTER NINE

# WHEN IRAN GET'S THE NUCLEAR BOMB!

Now please, because the word of God has to be understood, by those who are saved by God's grace, since the Holy Spirit, is the author of the word of God, he has to give understanding, because the word of God is written in a puzzle form, so that the lost people can't know what God is saying, and it takes the Holy Spirit to interpret it, and Since he will not indwell a lost person, they cannot understand the word of God, that is why, a great Sword, would, or could be a great weapon of war, such as a tank, *(__Unheard of in Ezekiel's day__)* God knew about the weapons of war we have today, bombs, Rifles, pistols, trucks, jeeps, since the latest writers of God's, word, lived on this earth, approximately 2000, years ago, they couldn't understand the modern day weapons, preachers in the 1900's didn't understand about the modern day weapons, that the countries of today have, or are attempting to get, and the prophet Ezekiel did not, and most likely, it would take too long, to explain it to the Apostle John, or Ezekiel, or any other writer of God's word, it wasn't meant to be in that day, that God's people could understand it.

Iran, will at least attempt to bomb Israel, in the attempt to destroy it, but Israel will in no doubt retaliate, because it has to defend itself against it's enemies, and when Israel Bombs Iran, then look out, the nations of the world, will unite to destroy that little Satan, as Iran calls them, as well as the United States, the big Satan, there will be war, pushed by the UN, because the UN hates Israel, every time, that Israel defends herself, against terrorism, of other countries against Israel, the UN always blames Israel, and always puts sanctions, against Israel, because the real Satan hates Israel, for the reason, that God still loves Israel, and always will, God said that he has turned his back on Israel but for a moment, and America, is now believing the lie, that God has replaced Israel with the church, and some churches subscribe to this great lie of the devil, the replacement theory, is a great lie of Satan, who hates Israel, and leads nations in that same great hate, and the UN, is also pushing a multitude of sanctions against Israel, for simply defending herself against her enemies. When Iran finally develops nuclear weapons, they will use them against Israel, and Israel will most definitely retaliate, with a nuclear bomb, which will incite the countries of the world, because of the pushing of the UN to do so. This only lines up with the word of God, many Christians of today will look at someone, as if they think them crazy, to tell them that Israel will be the target of the UN, and the league of nations, that make up the UN, such as Russia, Germany, France, England, Balkan nations, Poland, and satellite nations of Russia, and the word of God, tells us who will come against Israel, because Israel simply defended itself, by bombing Iran. The truth of the matter, is this, God will see to it that Israel is not wiped out, and will bless any nation that stands with Israel, he has promised this in his Word, not only will he bless nations that bless Israel, he will also bless individuals that bless Israel. The promise made to Abraham, Isaac, Jacob, and Jacob's descendants, still holds true, and you most likely have witnessed it.

***Genesis 12:3*** *"And I will bless them that bless thee, and curse him that curseth thee: and in thee shall all the families of the earth be blessed."*

The day before ***Hurricane Katrina, the USA*** and other countries, with the ok from the UN, there was an agreement made, by the Palestinians, plus the UN, plus the USA as they forced Israel to give up the Gaza strip, to Esau's descendants, when the Gaza strip, belonged to the descendants of Juda, but to the unlearned, this was the right thing to do, and at the time, I asked this question, Is the Hurricane Katrina, the result of this, giving away, God's property to the heathen, A tropical ***depression 12 formed on August 23/2005***, when Israeli troops were acting on orders from Ariel Sharon, in the implementation of President Bush's ***"(Road map to peace")*** plan The Israeli troops were dragging off the Jewish settlers who refused to leave the Gaza, and then Hurricane Katrina hit a region that is home to one fourth, 1/4 of US oil Production at a time when Americans were feeling anxiety over rising oil prices, and the storm hit a city making preparations for a big event glorifying a lifestyle, linking it to Sodom and Gomorrah, which was this, the 34th annual Southern Decadence 2005 festival, which evolved over the years from a party for a few friends to a six day street party attended by more than 100,000, people which runs from August 31-September 5th unoffically dubbed the ***"Gay Mardi Gras,"*** and when Katrina hit the USA, Oil prices jumped to $ 70.00 a barrel, prices for food also raised, as well as other Commodities, that must be trucked in, and many businesses went under, because of the rising prices of everything.

God help us all, we as the children of God ought to pay attention to God's warning, and promises to Israel, starting with Abraham, and handed down to Isaac, then to Jacob, and to Jacob's descendants, from Almighty God.

***Genesis 12:2,3—[2]*** *"And I will make thee a great nation, and I will bless thee, and make thy name great; and thou shalt be a blessing", **And I will bless them that bless thee, and curse him that curseth thee**: and in thee shall all the families of the earth be blessed."*

And the good old USA has suffered the results of the stealing of Israel's land and giving it to those who hate God, and hate Israel.

And in the book of ***Zephaniah***, we find a prediction, that we saw come true.

***Zephaniah 2:4*** *"For Gaza shall be forsaken, and Ashkelon a desolation: they shall drive out Ashdod at the noon day, and Ekron shall be rooted up."*

And it happened just exactly as God promised in Zephaniah, exactly at noon on the day of August 23/ 2005/ when the Israeli, troops were dragging out of Gaza, the last Israeli, settlers living there, and Hurricane Katrina, that hit the USA cost us billions of dollars, and it all could have been avoided, but God's people were, and it seems, are still asleep at the switch, and we can only blame it on us.

***2ⁿᵈ Chronicles 7:14*** *"If my people, which are called by my name, shall humble themselves, and pray, and seek my face, and turn from their wicked ways; then will I hear from heaven, and will forgive their sin, and will heal their land."*

That promise is also to us, he said if my people, which is every born again, person, shall humble ourselves, and pray, and he was not speaking of a "now lay me down to sleep kind of prayer", but one that would get God's attention, "And Seek My Face". this means, for us to ask the Lord, What would you have me to do Lord? And turn from our wicked ways, yes we all have wicked ways, why? Because we all inherited the same sinful nature from our forefather Adam.

I know that this not speaking of world War three, but I am attempting to get all who read this, to realize the importance, that Israel is, to Almighty God.

This promise has been passed down to all ages, since that promise was given, to Abraham, and it will remain through out the ages, handed down to Isaac, Jacob, and Jacob's descendants.

***Ecclesiates 3:14*** *"I know that, whatsoever God doeth, it shall be for ever: nothing can be put to it, nor any thing taken from it: and God doeth it, that man should fear before him."*

***Psalms 122: 6*** *"Pray for the peace of Jerusalem: they shall prosper that love thee."*

This is a great promise from God, to all that will love Israel. It is a promise to all, who will love Israel, the blessings of God upon them.

If you will turn to ***Ezekiel 38,39,*** you will find a promise of a great war, that has never happened as of yet, and it is not the battle of Armageddon, neither is it the war that takes place after the reign of Christ, for in both of these wars, the opposing armies that come against Israel, will be completely destroyed .At Armageddon, Jesus Christ will completely destroy all the armies that come against Israel, and after the reign of Christ is over when Satan is released, out of the bottomless pit, and gathers a great army that comes against Israel, then God rains down fire and brimstone and destroys all of this army, then Satan is cast into the lake of fire and brimstone, but the war that Ezekiel describes, **one sixth of this army that comes against Israel, will be allowed to live, and return home,** *(Remember, If I repeat these verses of scripture, and explanations, I'm trying to get the reader to understand, what is taking place)*

**Ezekiel 39:2** *"And I will turn thee back, and leave but the sixth part of thee, and will cause thee to come up from the north parts, and will bring thee upon the mountains of Israel:"*

This has not happened, but will happen soon, just after the Rapture of the Church, and by it the Beast, Anti-christ, will gain his great power, How? you might ask, by winning this great war, by rescuing Israel from it's enemies, and you might say, that God could do this, by his word, yes he could, but he will let the anti-christ win, this war to fulfill his word by putting the anti-christ to the position where he will be that ***Strong Delusion*** that God has promised he would send to all who have heard the gospel, and decided they didn't want, or didn't need the salvation of the Lord. You might also ask, How do you know this? Well God reveals a lot of things to those that fear him. And that studies his word.

**2nd Thessalonians 2:9-12—[9]** *"Even him, whose coming is after the working of Satan with all power and signs and lying wonders."*
*[10] "And with all deceivableness of unrighteousness in them that perish; because they received not the love of the truth, that they might be saved."*

*[11] "And for this cause God shall send them strong delusion, that they should believe a lie:"*

*[12] "That they all might be damned who believed not the truth, but had pleasure in unrighteousness."*

*Psalms 25:14 "The secret of the LORD is with them that fear him; and he will shew them his covenant."*

*Ezekiel 38:1-6—[1] "AND the word of God came unto me, saying,"*

*[2] "Son of man, set thy face against Gog, the land of Magog, the chief prince of Meshech and Tubal, and prophesy against him."*

Let me pause here for just a little while and see what God is beginning to tell us, son of man set thy face against the devil, for he is the prince of Magog, known here as Gog, and prophesy against him. Meshech, and Tubal, is Moscow, and Tobolsk in the land of Russia.

*[3] "And say, Thus saith the Lord GOD; behold, I am against thee, O Gog, the chief prince of Meshech and Tubal:"*

*[4] "And I will turn thee back, and put hooks into thy jaws, and I will bring thee forth, and thine army, horses and horsemen, all of them clothed with all sorts of Armour, even a great company with bucklers and shields, all of them handling swords:"*

Horses, and Horsemen, could be a symbol of the transportation of today, for the mention of tanks, and cars, would be something that could not be understood, by the Old Testament prophets, or even the New Testament Apostles, the weapons, of war that the world has today, would be not understood, even by the people of the early 1900's when the Nuclear bomb, was first manufactured, there were millions of people, that didn't understand, about these weapons of war

A sword in the Old Testament times, was best known as a weapon of war, and the sword stands for any kind of weapon, in **Revelation 6: 4**, because in Ezekiel's time, it was unheard of, such as a rifle, or tank, or any modern day kind of weapon, as a matter of fact, a bomb of any kind was unheard of, much, much later, in time, was black powder discovered in China.

God says I'm sending you against Israel, talking to Gog the chief prince of Magog, because they have bombed Iran, and stopped the flow of oil, you see this is God's purpose, to let the beast, or anti-christ, rescue Israel, from destruction, by this great army, that Russia, is going to bring against Israel, for it is because the beast is meant to be the strong delusion, that God has promised, he would send to this earth, after the church is called out of this world, and God will use the beast, to deceive those who refused, the Lord Jesus Christ as their Saviour.

*[5] "Persia, Ethiopia, and Libya, with them; all of them with shield and helmet."*
*[6] "Gomer, and all his bands; the house of Togarmah of the north quarters, and all his bands: and many people with thee."*

*Persia,* is the modern day *Iran,* and *Syria,* and *Ethiopia,* as well as *Libya*, are from the northern part of *Africa,* the house of *Togarmah, is Poland*, and the *Bulgarian nations, Gomer is Germany, France, Great Britain, and other nations that have the ancestral people that are descendants of Japheth.*

Study——— *Genesis 10: 1-5—[1] "NOW these are the Generations of the sons of Noah, Shem, Ham, and Japheth: and unto them were sons born after the flood."*
*[2] "The sons of Japheth: Gomer, and Magog, and Madai, and Javan, and Tubal, and Meshech, and Tiras."*

*Gomer* settled in the land of the European nations that are made up of white people, such as Germany, France, England, Norway, Sweden, and all the Celtic nations. *Magog* settled in the now known land of Russia the land of the ancient Scythians, or Tartars, whose descendants are people predominately in the modern day Russia. *Madai* fathered the ancient Medes. *Javan* settled in the land of Greece, and Syria, *Tubal* descendants settled, most likely in Tobolsk, and got it's name from him, and a part of those descendants also populated Spain. *Meshech* also of modern day Russia. *Tiras* the father of the Thracians. These were the seven sons of Japheth, Noah's eldest son, this is where they settled after the flood, when God divided the people, with different languages, when they were attempting to build a tower into heaven, found in the ___11ᵗʰ Chapter of Genesis.___

___Genesis 11:5-9—[5]___ *"And the LORD came down to see the city and the tower, which the children of men builded."*
*[6] "And the LORD said, Behold, the people is one, and they have all one language; and this they begin to do: and now nothing will be restrained from them, which they have imagined to do."*
*[7] "Go to, let us go down, and there confound their language, that they may not understand one another's speech."*
*[8] "So the LORD scattered them abroad from thence upon the face of all the earth: and they left off to build the city."*
*[9] "Therefore is the name of it called Babel; because the LORD did there confound the language of all the earth: and from thence did the LORD scatter them abroad upon the face of all the earth."*

The following is the reason that I say that God will let the anti-christ, or the beast, rescue Israel, from this great multitude of the Russian army, that comes against Israel, to cause multitudes to believe that he is the Messiah who was promised to come, Especially, most of them will accept him as the Messiah, because the people of the world will believe that only God could do what he has accomplished, and it is true, but God does it through the beast to fulfill his word. Two thirds of Israel will accept the Mark of the beast, and doom their souls, thinking he is the Messiah, they have been looking for. Israel is beloved of God, but not all Israel is Israel, and to understand that statement, is to understand, what the Name Israel means, and the name means(A Prince with God)

___Romans 9:6,7—[6]___ *"Not as though the word of God hath taken none effect. For they are not all Israel, which are of Israel:"*
*[7] "Neither, because they are the seed of Abraham, are they all children: but, In Isaac shall thy seed be called."*

When you might think of Israel, you might think of all of the people of Israel, but in the last half of the Seven Years of the Great Tribulation Period, there will be two Thirds of the people of Israel, will accept the Mark of the Beast and doom their souls to a devil's hell, and those people, are not the Children of Israel, spiritually called (A Prince with God), For they are Traitors to the Living God, the same as those who rejected the Truth, when He came to this earth, approximately two thousand years ago, give or take a few years, or so. And according to God's word, not all Israel is Israel, and it makes sense, when we understand, what the word (Israel) means.

*Zechariah 13:8,9—[8] "And it shall come to pass, that in all the land, (Israel) saith the LORD, two parts therein shall be cut off and die; but the third shall be left therein."*
*[9] "And I will bring the third part through the fire, (Tribulation) and will refine them as silver is refined, and will try them as gold is tried: they shall call on my name, and I will hear them: I will say, It is my people: and they shall say, The LORD is my God."*

And here is the reason, I say that they2/3of Israel, plus multitudes of other people will believe that he is the Messiah, that was Promised to come, and Israel didn't accept him, when the true Messiah came, they are still looking for him.

*Revelation 13:4 "And they worshipped the dragon which gave power unto the beast, and they worshipped the beast, saying, Who is able to make war with him?"*

*Daniel 12:7 "And I heard the man clothed in linen, which was upon the waters of the river, when he held up his right hand and his left hand unto heaven, and sware by him that liveth for ever that it shall be for a time, (year) times, (two years), and a half; (6 months) and when he shall have accomplished to scatter the power of the holy people, (Israel) all these things shall be finished."*

By destroying this mighty army, that is led by Russia, it will be so spectacular, that two thirds of Israel will believe that only God could accomplish this, and two thirds of Israel, and the majority of the world, will take the mark of the beast, believing this is the Messiah, that they have been looking for so long, and doom their souls to hell and the lake of fire, but one third of Israel, will refuse the mark of the beast, because they will have listened to the 144,000 preachers that were sealed in **_Revelation 7ᵗʰ Chapter_**, but the 144,000 preachers will be beheaded because of their preaching, against the anti-christ, or beast, the usage of the word (Beast) by God, we get the sense, of him being of a beastly nature, no Conscience of right and wrong, and what he wants, is all there is to him, that is why God refers to him as a beast. For no doubt, he will be a very handsome man, in the eyes of people, for people can't see the heart of the man.

The rescuing of Israel from this massive army, will be so spectacular, that people will believe that only God could do such a feat as this.

And here is the reason I say that the beast, or anti-christ will be that strong delusion, that God has promised to send to all who refused to accept the gospel, of the Lord Jesus Christ.

**_2ⁿᵈ Thessalonians 2:9-12—[9] "Even him, (anti-christ) whose coming is after the working of Satan with all power and signs and lying wonders."_**
**_[10] "And with all deceivableness of unrighteousness in them that perish; because they received not the love of the truth, that they might be saved."_**
**_[11] "And for this cause God shall send them strong delusion, that they should believe a lie:"_**
**_[12] "That they all might be damned who believed not the truth, but had pleasure in unrighteousness."_**

What could be more of a strong delusion, than, the anti-christ rescuing Israel from this massive army, that comes against Israel???? He is the beast that rises out of the sea, (Sea of humanity) in———,

**_Revelation 13:1 "AND I stood upon the sand of the sea, (sea of humanity) and saw a beast rise up out of the sea, ( again the sea of humanity) having seven heads and ten horns, and upon his horns ten crowns, and upon his heads the name of blasphemy."_**

Let me stop here and explain this verse of scripture, the seven heads, are the seven Emperors of Rome, that God takes a particular interest in, for the seven are the most wicked of them all, and according to History, there are many more Emperors of Rome, all were wicked, yet none as the Seven he is speaking of, and the last one being Constantine, who was also the first Pope of Rome, and the word of God states that the beast will be the eighth, also HORNS always represent kingdoms, and he will hold power over ten kingdoms, and upon his heads the name of Blasphemy, meaning the world will proclaim, that he is the Messiah, and in the middle of the seven year Tribulation Period, he will proclaim, that he is the Messiah, and demand worship, from all people.

*Revelation 13: 2 "And the beast which I saw was like unto a leopard, and his feet were as the feet of a bear, and his mouth as the mouth of a lion: and the dragon gave him his power, and his seat, and great authority."*

Again let stop here and explain this verse of scripture, so as not to let any one to be confused. And perhaps, I will stop at each verse and explain.

His appearance was like unto a Leopard, he is empowered by Satan, who gives him the power of the of the Greek Empire, of Alexander the Great, who was represented as swift as a leopard,, and he had the feet of a Bear, and again Satan gives him the power, and appearance of the Empire of the Medes and the Persians, which is described as a bear, in ***Daniel***, and he had the mouth of the Lion, again Satan gives him the power of the Babylonian Empire, under Nebchadnezzar, and he will be like the old Roman Empire, as seen by Daniel, with feet as iron and of clay, which will not mix, but will be divided somewhat.

*Revelation 13:3 "And I saw one of his heads as it were wounded to death; and his deadly wound was healed: and all the world wondered after the beast."*

One head was The old Roman Empire and was wounded to death, when Constantine was Emperor, he saw his kingdom slipping away, so he let the Roman Empire die, and put on the robes of the Catholic church, as the first Pope, this was about 316 AD, the idea began in the church of **_Ephesians,_** and was not accepted there, but was began stronger in the church of **_Pergamos,_** and became much stronger in the church of **_Thyatira,_** AD 500 AD. **_Nicolatanes,_** which was a priestly order, that was rejected in the church of the Ephesians but accepted in the church of Pergamos, approximately 316 AD.

**_Revelation 13:4 "And they worshipped the dragon which gave power unto the beast: and they worshipped the beast, saying Who is like unto the beast? Who is able to make war with him?"_**

This is when the beast wins the war, against, this great army led by Russia, and the people will think that only God could accomplish, this great task, this is how they worship the devil, who gives power to the beast, and they worship the beast, saying who is like unto the beast, and who can make war against him?

**_Revelation 13:5 "And there was given unto him a mouth speaking great things and blasphemies; and power was given unto him to continue forty and two months."_**

This begins in the middle of the seven years of Great Tribulation period, when the beast moves into the temple in Jerusalem, and declares that he is God, and demand worship form all the world, also this is when God hides the Remnant of Israel, the one third, who refuse to accept the mark of the Beast. Who have listened to the preaching of the 144,000 preachers, ordained in **_Revelation 7_**

**_Isaiah 16:4 "Let mine outcasts dwell with thee, Moab: be thou a covert to them from the face of the spoiler: for the extortioner is at end, the spoiler ceaseth, the oppressors are consumed out of the land."_**

Moab a small country settled by the eldest son of Lot, after he was conceived by incest, of Lot and his eldest daughter, when they fled the destruction of Sodom. This Moab is found in the modern day of Jordan. This is where the Lord will hide the remnant of Israel, during the last half of the seven years of Great Tribulation period.. And when they get to Moab, nothing can touch them, for Moab and Edom, and Ammon, are the three countries, that the beast can't touch, they are kept from his hands, but kept in the hands of Almighty God.

*Matthew 24:15-26—[15]* *"When ye therefore shall see the abomination of desolation, spoken of by Daniel the prophet, stand in the holy place, (whoso readeth, let him understand.) [16] "Then let them which be in Judaea flee into the mountains:"*

This is when Jesus warns the remnant to flee into the mountains of Moab, when the anti-christ moves into the temple in Jerusalem, and demands worship, from all the world.

*[17] "Let him which is on the housetop not come down to take any thing out of his house."*

Leave immediately, as you are, was his warning, by doing anything else endangers their very life, for the beast will surely attempt to kill all of the remnant of Israel, who refuse to take his mark, or worship him. There are also others, who will refuse the Mark of the beast, and no doubt, they will have heard the preaching of the 144,000, Israeli preachers, and this will make the beast, very angry, desiring to kill all of his enemies, for they are a threat to him, that is in his mind, and remember, he is just fulfilling God's word, and when God gets through with him, he will be thrown into the Lake of Fire, along with the false Prophet.

*[18] "Neither let him which is in the field return back to take his clothes."*
*[19] "And woe unto them that are with child, and to them that give suck in those days."*

This is a stern warning to the women, who are with child, or those who will have very small children, for it will be that, they will almost starve, and perhaps the very small children will starve, because the mother will not have enough nourishment, to supply milk for their little ones. Nor food, for those children, who are too old to receive nourishment from their mothers.

**[20] "But pray ye that you flight be not in the winter, neither on the sabbath day:"**

At this time the Old testament law of the Sabbath day, will be back in force, and on the Sabbath day the children of Israel were not allowed to go more than, an half, to three quarters of a mile from home, on the Sabbath day. And if they travel to Moab, it will be the breaking of the law of Moses, and now in our time, there are priest in Israel, studying the Old Testament law, until the first three and one half years of the Great Tribulation period, and the anti-christ will reinstate the priest, and the use of the Old Testament Mosaic law, but in the last three and one half years, when the beast takes over the Temple in Jerusalem, and demands every person on earth to worship him, and this is when God instructs the Remnant of Israel, and perhaps the remnant of Egypt, and the remnant of Assyria to flee into Moab, and in the winter time, it will be very rough on them, and some might freeze, and others might catch bad colds, or worse. And in their weaken system, they might take Pneumonia, and might die, and God wants them to make it to Moab, where they will be taken care of.

**_Daniel 9:27_ "And he (beast) shall confirm the covenant with many for one week:(seven years) and in the midst of the week he shall cause the sacrifice and the oblation to cease, and for the overspreading of abominations he shall make it desolate, even until the consummnation, and that determined shall be poured upon the desolate."**

This is when the beast will make a covenant with Israel, to reinstate the Old Testament law, of worship, of sacrificing of animals and the overspreading of abominations, will be in the middle of the seven years of great Tribulation period, when he claims all the temple in Jerusalem, and declare he is the Messiah, and demand worship, of all the people.

**_Matthew 24:21_ "For then shall be great tribulation, such as was not since the beginning of the world to this time, no, nor ever shall be."**

This great Tribulation, that will be worse than anything, ever before, or after, is when the beast, or anti-christ, moves into the Temple and claims to be the Messiah, and God starts pouring out his wrath on the earth.

God warns the remnant that it will be a time worse than there ever has been, a time of great tribulation, when they will be hunted by the forces of the beast, to hunt and destroy, because they are guilty of treason to the beast, and the penalty if caught, will be death.

God always takes care of those that trust him, when Elijah was on earth, and thought that all the people of God, had been killed, and he was the only one left, he spoke to God, that all the prophets had been killed, and he was left alone, then God answered him, with this,—

*Romans 11:1-5—[1] "I SAY then, Hath God cast away his people? God forbid. For I also am an Israelite, of the seed of Abraham, of the tribe of Benjamin."*
*[2] "God hath not cast away his people which he foreknew, Wot ye not what the scripture saith of Elias? How he maketh intercession to God against Irael, saying,"*
*[3] "Lord, they have killed thy prophets, and digged down thine altars; and I am left alone, and they seek my life."*
*[4] "But what saith the answer of God to him? I have reserved to myself seven thousand men, who have not bowed the knee to the image of Baal."*
*[5] "Even so then at this present time also there is a remnant according to the election of grace."*

also you can find this in———————-.

*1ˢᵗ Kings 19:14-18.—[14] "And he said, I have been very jealous for the LORD God of hosts: because the children of Israel have forsaken thy covenant, thrown down thine altars, and slain thy prophets with the sword; and I, even I only, am left; and they seek my life, to take it away."*
*[15] "And the LORD said unto him, Go, return on thy way to the wilderness of Damascus: and when thou comest, anoint Hazael to be king over Syria:"*

*[16] "And Jehu the son of Nimshi shalt thou anoint to be king over Israel: and Elisha the son of Shaphat of Abel-meholah shalt thou anoint to be prophet in thy room."*

*[17] "And it shall come to pass, that him that escapeth the sword of Hazael shall Jehu slay: and him that escapeth from the sword of Jehu shall Elisha slay."*

*[18] "Yet I have left me seven thousand in Israel, all the knees which have not bowed unto Baal, and every mouth which hath not kissed him."*

Let me attempt to explain, these verses of scripture, if I may, for I'm setting up the History of Israel at a time, when Elijah got discouraged and wanted to Lord to just kill him, and take him out of this world, to escape the trouble in Israel, Elijah believing that all Israel had turned against God, and was hunting him to kill him also, but God told this discouraged Prophet, that there was seven thousand men, that had not turned their backs on God, and were still faithful to God. Now let's get back to————

## Matthew 24: 22- 26

*[22] "And except those days should be shortened, there should no flesh be saved: but for the elect's sake those days shall be shortened."*

Let me attempt to explain, what is meant by the word Elect, or Election, and it means according to the foreknowledge of God, **meaning**, God knows all things, and he knows who will trust him, from before the time, that he created the earth, and all the universe, he knew you, and he knew me, and he knew who would reject him, and he knew who would accept him, there is no stopping point to God's knowledge, he knew me, and he knew the day that I would call upon him to save my soul, and he know's all about you as well. There is nothing that can be hid from God, he knows all, and he sees all.

The Lord will see to it, that all the remnant will be spared, because these are the elect, the remnant of Israel. *Also, The remnant of Egypt, the remnant of Assyria, to find this out, go to Isaiah 19:19-25.*

**_Matthew 24: 23_** *"Then if any man shall say unto you, Lo, here is Christ, or there ; believe it not."*

For Christ will not have returned in power and great glory at this time, and if any say he is here, or there, they are wrong, or lying. But there are false Christs even today, I could name you at least one, and he says that his third wife, is the Holy Spirit, and this is what God warns all to reject, for they lie, and they are of their father the devil, as the Lord warns people of before he left this earth, the first time.

**_John 8:44_** *"Ye are of your father the devil, and the lusts of your father ye will do. He was a murderer from the beginning, and abode not in the truth, because there is no truth in him.*
*[45] "When he speaketh a lie, he speaketh of his own: for he is a liar, and the father of it."*

This was how Lucifer got to be the devil, by his lusts, he wanted to be a god, but got kicked out of heaven, and one third of the angels, who followed him, were cast into hell, where they await, the Great White Throne Judgment of God, where they will be tried, and cast into the Lake of fire, and God has reserved four of the fallen angels, to work in the time of the Great Tribulation Period. he saw how the angels, worshiped God, (the lust of the eye) and he desired the same, (the lust of the flesh) and he was the strongest angel, and the most beautiful angel in heaven, so he thought he would just take it (The pride of life), this was what got his comeuppance, and that is what he uses on humans, for it worked on him, and brought destruction, to his greatness, and the same works on humans today. *(Now back to Matthew 24:)*————————————,

*[24] "For there shall arise false Christs, and false prophets, and shall shew great signs and wonders ; insomuch that, if it were possible, they shall deceive the very elect."*

At this time the elect will be so tired from their journey, that they might be easily deceived into thinking, no harm can come to them, because of these who claim to be Christ, but are not, so Jesus warns them ahead of the time. So that they will be aware, of what is ahead of them, if they fail to watch, and depend upon him, instead of false Christ's.

*[25] "Behold, I have told you before."*
*[26] "Wherefore if they shall say unto you, Behold, he is in the desert; go not forth: behold, he is in the secret chambers; believe it not."*

No doubt there will be those who will attempt to betray the remnant, for a reward, might be offered, for their capture.

Now let's go back to ***Revelation 13<sup>th</sup> chapter***, and continue our study on the beast, or antichrist, which ever name you might use, or choose.

***Revelation 13:6 [6] "And he opened his mouth in blasphemy against God, to blaspheme his name, and his tabernacle, and them that dwell in heaven."***

This is the time when the Lord Jesus, opens the seventh seal, and when the beast moves into the temple in Jerusalem, and declares he is God, and demands worship from every human being, on earth.

***Revelation 8:1 "AND when he had opened the seventh seal, there was silence in heaven about the space of half an hour."***

No doubt the angels, and the Saints that are in heaven, will hold their breath, when they witness this terrible blasphemy coming from a mere man, claiming to be the Christ, and perhaps wondering what God was going to do about it, there are certain people today that claim to be the Christ, but it seems they are short lived.

***Revelation 13:7 "And it was given unto him( the beast) to make war with the saints, and to overcome them: and power was given him over all kindreds, and tongues, and nations."***

This is where he has the 144,000, beheaded, because of their preaching against him, and proclaiming that he is an imposter, and not the true Messiah and he is given the office of Emperor of the world like unto the old Roman Empire, where everyone was supposed to worship, the Emperor.

***Revelation 13:8*** *"And all that dwell upon the earth shall worship him, whose names are not written in the book of life of the Lamb slain from the foundation of the world."*

And all mankind, upon the earth at this time will worship him(the beast) whose names are not written in the Lambs book of life from the foundation of the world, it was according to the foreknowledge of God who would worship the Lord Jesus Christ, and those as well, that would worship the beast, and in that determinate council, of God the Father, God the Son, and God the Holy Spirit, that one of them would have come to this earth and die, a terrible death, and shed his blood to redeem mankind back to God, and it was determined that God the Son, The Word, would come to this earth and redeem fallen man, and it was written down in the Lamb's book of life, before the foundation of the world, who would accept the true God, and who would not, according to the foreknowledge of God, and the ones who would accept the salvation of God, their names were written down in the Lamb's book of life at that time.

***Revelation 13:9*** *"If any have an ear, let him hear."*

This a warning from Almighty God, for every man, woman, boy, or girl to listen to God's word, and take heed to it. Then there is the other beast out of the earth, having two horns, like a lamb. But sold out to the devil, to revel in the power of the first beast, and to go about bring the first beast into that power. Which will be the head, or the power of the Great Whore told about in ***Revelation 17:1-14—[1]*** *"AND there came one of the seven angels which had the seven vials, and talked with me, saying unto me, Come hither; I will shew unto thee the judgement of the great whore that sitteth upon many waters:"*
*[2] With whom the kings of the earth have committed fornication, and the inhabitants of the earth have been made drunk with the wine of her fornication."*
*[3] "So he carried me away in the spirit into the wilderness: and I saw a woman sit upon a scarlet coloured beast, full of names of blasphemy, having seven heads and ten horns."*

A religion in the word of God is always addressed as a female, and this is how this religion is spoken of. An unfaithful, or a perverted female.

Here the Lord calls this creature sitting upon a scarlet colored beast, he says that it is a woman, and he calls her a whore, a religion with great riches, and the woman, which represents a false religion, and this false religion, helps the beast to get into power, and perhaps you've seen pictures of this beast, and it has seven heads, but this beast has one head, but represents, the old Roman Empire, as another Emperor the seven heads represents the seven, Emperors of Rome, that were the most evil, and Constantine which was the last Emperor, but he saw his Empire slipping away from him, the loose living of all the people, caused the empire to become weak, so before this, he went into Turkey to defeat the other Empire, the Roman Empire, was divided, into two parts, one part in Turkey, the other in Rome. One was in ___**Instanbul, Turkey**___, and the other in ___**Rome Italy,**___

Constantine, on his way to Turkey claimed he saw the sign of a cross in the sky, and he made all his soldiers paint a cross on their shields, and baptized each one, then proceeded to I*nstanbul* to fight against the Emperor there, and won the victory, and renamed ___**Instanbul, Turkey**___, to be ___**Constantinople, Turkey**___. After returning to Rome, he saw his kingdom getting weaker, and weaker, so he decided to change his Emperor robes, to the Robes of a high Priest, and became the first Pope of Rome, and you can find this in the annals of history, one of the history books you can find this, is in——-___**The Two Babylons**___, by Alexander Hyslop.

___**Revelation 17:5**___ ___*"And upon her forehead was a name written, MYSTERY, BABYLON THE GREAT, THE MOTHER OF HARLOTS AND ABOMINATIONS OF THE EARTH."*___

This is a great indictment from the Lord Jesus Christ against this religion, and later he even tells where her headquarters is found. And the head of this religion, is where the false prophet comes in, and he helps the beast to get into power, and finally the beast destroys this religion. By using these ten kings, that give themselves to the beast.

***Revelation 17:6*** *"And I saw the woman drunken with the blood of the saints, and with the blood of the martyrs of Jesus: and when I saw her, I wondered with great admiration."*

Until the year 1980, according to a former Jesuit Priest, "ALBERTO RIVERIA", tells of the record kept by this religion, they burned at the stake, and by other means of torture, killed, over 61 million Christians. Also read, "***FOXES book of Martyrs***".

*[7] "And the angel said unto me, Wherefore didst thou marvel? I will tell thee the mystery of the woman, and of the beast that carrieth her, which hath the seven heads and ten horns."*
*[8] "The beast that thou sawest was, and is not; and shall ascend into perdition: and they that dwell on the earth shall wonder, whose names were not written in the book of life from the foundation of the world, when they behold the beast that was, and is not, and yet is."*

Let me stop here and attempt to explain, the beast that was, and is not, and yet is, he will be no doubt a handsome man, a man with much Charm, yet having a beastly nature, no feeling for human life, or anything else, just the lust for great power.

*[9] "And here is the mind which hath wisdom. The seven heads are seven mountains on which the woman sitteth."*

There is only one place known for it's seven hills, and it is the Vatican, in Rome Italy.

*[10] "And there are seven kings: five are fallen, and one is, and the other is not yet come; and when he cometh, he must continue a short space."* *(Constantine)*
*[11] "And the beast that was, and is not, even he is the eighth, and is of the seven, and goeth into perdition."* The beast will be as one of the other seven Emperors of Rome

According to History there were more than seven Emperors of Rome, but these seven, are the ones that God is paying attention to, ***Number {7}*** was Constantine who quit the Roman Empire, and traded his robes, of the Empire, for the robes of the first Pope. As was told by a former Jesuit Priest, who got saved by God's grace, and quit the Catholic church, his name was Alberto Riveria.

*[12] "And the ten horns which thou sawest are ten kings, which have received no kingdom as yet; but receive power as kings one hour with the beast."*
*[13] "These have one mind, and shall give their power and strength unto the beast."*
*[14] "These shall make war with the Lamb, and the Lamb shall overcome them: for he is Lord of Lords, and King of kings: and they that are with him are called, and chosen and faithful."*

This verse fourteen, speaks of the battle of Armageddon, when the Lord comes back, and sets up his throne, and judges the nations, as to how each nation has treated Israel, and the church, and the nations that have been cruel to Israel and the church, will not be a nation in the kingdom of Christ. But the nations that have been good to Israel, and the church, will be nations in Christ's kingdom.

Some of this is recorded, by others and retold by me, as far as the last Emperor, Constantine, I just repeat what I've read, and can't swear to the accuracy, of it, but as the accuracy of the scriptures, it is proven over and over .

The following speaks of the false prophet, and all these things line up to tell us more about this war, which will be world war three, a Nuclear war, some say it will be a one day war, but I'm somewhat skeptical, of that, there are too many people involved, to make it a one day war, but I agree, it will be a short war, so that all things, the Lord predicted, would happen, can happen.

It will be a short war, to fulfill God'sword, as to the strong delusion, spoken of in————-,

**2ⁿᵈ *Corinthians 2:9-12,*** and the Beast, or anti-christ will be that Strong delusion.

# CHAPTER TEN

# *THE FALSE PROPHET*

*Revelation 13:11-18—[11] "And I beheld another beast coming up out of the earth; and he had two horns like a lamb, and he spake as a dragon."*
*[12] "And he exerciseth all the power of the first beast before him, and causeth the earth and them which dwell therein to worship the first beast, whose deadly wound was healed."*
*[13] "And he doth great wonders, so that he maketh fire come down from heaven on the earth in the sight of men."*

Here the false prophet, is giving an imitation of the prophet Elijah, who called fire down from heaven, and destroyed the armies of fifty, and you can be sure of one thing, the devil knows scripture, or, how else can he deceive so many people, the false prophet is attempting to fulfill, these scriptures, found in the book of Malachi, and you might ask, how does he call fire down from heaven? Well, by Satellite, is how.

*Malachi 4:5,6—[5] "Behold, I will send you Elijah the prophet before the coming of the great and dreadful day of the LORD:"*
*[6] "And he shall turn the heart of the fathers to the children, and the heart of the children to their fathers, lest I come and smite the earth with a curse."*

So if some know the scriptures, they will think that this is Elijah, and he would point to only the Messiah, and when he points to the beast, or anti-christ, they will follow his lead, because they are not saved, even if they know some scriptures.

***Revelation 13:14-18—[14]*** *"And deceiveth them that dwell on the earth by means of those miracles which he had power to do in the sight of the beast; saying to them that dwell on the earth, that they should make an image to the beast, which had the wound by a sword, and did live."*

Some say it will be Nero, and some say it will be John F. Kennedy, because he was shot in the head, and some say it will be Ronald Wilson Reagan, because the letters in his name amount to 666, Ronald, 6 letters, Wilson, 6 letters, Reagan, 6 letters, but regardless of all this, If He is in heaven, he surely would not come to the earth, and be that strong Delusion, and if he was in hell, I'm sure, he'd be telling every one who was the real Christ, so there must be another explanation, to this question.

So to me, it must be a man, who will be wounded, and live, as the word of God states, even if he is a mystery, the wound by the sword, should not be such a mystery. It might be a terrible wound, and yet he survives, but God's word is true, and that is for sure.

***Revelation 13:15*** *"And he had power to give life unto the image of the beast, that the image of the beast should both speak, and cause that as many as would not worship the image of the beast should be killed."*

This could very well be a walking, talking computer, because the technology, of man today is very great, and to make a computer that could do all this, is not beyond the realm of mankind, of today.

***Revelation 13:6*** *"And causeth all, both small and great, rich and poor, free and bond, to receive a mark in their right hand, or in their foreheads:"*
***Revelation 13:7*** *"And that no man might buy or sell, save he that had the mark, or the name of the beast, or the number of his name."*

This could be done with scanners, such as grocery stores have to scan the prices of the items, they sell, so if a person went into a store to buy something, without the mark, they can't buy food, and no doubt would be reported to the authorities. And suffer the consequences, or accept the mark, and this all could very well be caused, by this great war, and everything has to be rationed.

*Revelation 6:5,6  [5] "And when he had opened the third seal, I heard the third beast say, Come and see. And I beheld, and lo a black horse; and he that sat on him had a pair of balances in his hand."*

The rationing of food stuffs, no doubt, will cause millions to starve, and no doubt, will cause the animal kingdom, to be viscous, and even kill humans, for food.

*[6] "And I heard a voice in the midst of the four beasts say, A measure of wheat for a penny, and three measures of barley for a penny; and see thou hurt not the oil and the wine."*

This announces a great famine, in all the world, no doubt caused by this great war, food stuffs, will be almost all wiped out, so every thing has to be rationed, and the mark of the beast, is the temporary measure, for people to buy food, but the mark dooms souls to hell, is the everlasting curse. The measure of wheat for a penny, and three measures of barley for a penny, in John's day, a penny was a day's wages, and a measure was just enough for one person's food.

*Revelation 13:18 "Here is wisdom. Let him that hath understanding count the number of the beast: for it is the number of a man; and his number is Six hundred three score and six."*

6 is the number of man, because God created man on the sixth day, so 666, is the ultimate in mankind's prosperity. So 666, is as highest, that is possible for man to acquire.

No doubt, the anti- christ, will be a genius, most likely educated in the most desirable school, of higher education. There are anti-christs in the world today, even some of our Christian Colleges, have professors, that are anti-christ, meaning, they don't even believe in the Lord Jesus Christ.

It is the ability, and influence of the false prophet, with the two horns like a lamb, that is able to deceive multiplied millions of people, into believing that the beast is the Messiah. One reason is the beast will be a great man of knowledge, and warfare, and all this because God sends this strong delusion, to millions, who have rejected the true Messiah.

*Ezekiel 38:7—11—[7] "Be thou prepared, and prepare for thyself, thou, and all thy company that are assembled unto thee, and be thou a guard unto them.*

*[8] "After many days thou shalt be visited: in the latter years thou shalt come into the land that is brought back from the sword, and is gathered out of many people, against the mountains of Israel, which have been always waste: but it is brought forth out of the nations, and they shall dwell safely all of them."*

*[9] "Thou shalt ascend and come like a storm, thou shalt be like a cloud to cover the land, thou, and all thy bands, and many people with thee."*

*[10] "Thus saith the Lord GOD; It shall also come to pass, that at the same time shall things come into thy mind, and thou shalt think an evil thought:"*

*[11] "And thou shalt say, I will go up to the land of unwalled villages; I will go to them that are at rest, that dwell safely, all of them dwelling without walls, and having neither bars nor gates."*

The phrase *The Lord GOD*, shows the Almighty God, the all powerful God, when in most of the Old Testament writings, it is as this, the **LORD God.**

That word found in verses **8,9,10 SHALT** is a word signifying something that has to be done, no way around it, it is more than the word **SHALL**, which means, used as an auxiliary to indicate futurity, determination or promise. According to Webster's dictionary.

*Ezekiel 38:12—18—[12] "To take a spoil, and to take a prey; to turn thine hand upon the desolate places that are now inhabited, and upon the people that are gathered out of the nations, which have gotten cattle and goods, that dwell in the midst of the land."*

As is stated in verse 11, we see that this great army will go up, so they must have come down from the North, down the Atlantic, and come into the Persian Gulf, because the next verse talks about Saudi Arabia, and Spain, so they must come down along the coast of the Atlantic, at least some of them, and disembark in the Mediterranean, then on to the Persian Gulf, and go north, here is where they gather some more to their army, the Saudi plus other Muslim terrorist, determined on destroying Israel. Because Israel has a lot of cattle, sheep, gold, silver, and other kinds of prey, now some of this might seem to be past tense, but you can be sure it is future tense. Russia has always wanted the warm ports of Israel, to ship out oil from the middle East, the Palestinians wants Israel land, but they will not get it, if Israel is destroyed, Russia will take the land, because of the chemical riches in the Dead Sea, and the Ports of the Mediterranean Sea, but Israel will never be destroyed, because the Land belongs to Almighty God, and God loves Israel, and will not let their land be taken by Russia, or any one else.

*[13] "Sheba, and Dedan, (Saudi Arabia) and the merchants of Tarshish, (Spain) with all the young lions thereof, (Militants) shall say unto thee, art thou come to take a spoil? Hast thou gathered thy company to take a prey? To carry away silver and gold, to take away cattle and goods, to take a great spoil?"*
*[14] "Therefore, son of man, prophesy and say unto Gog, thus saith the Lord GOD; In that day when my people of Israel dwelleth safely, Shalt thou not know it?"*

Or you will most certainly know it, without a doubt.

*[15] "And thou shalt come from thy place out of the north parts, thou and many people with thee, all of them riding upon horses, a great company, and a mighty army riding upon horses,"*
(Jeeps, and airplanes, and other means of transportation), which were unheard of in Ezekiel time, and God knew all about them, but

he also knew, when this was understood, people of the world, would also know about all means of transportation.

*[16] "And thou <u>shalt</u> come up against my people of Israel, as a cloud to cover the land; it shall be in the latter days, and I will bring thee against my land, that the heathen may know me, when I shall be sanctified in thee, O Gog, before their eyes."*

It don't say they will understand it, but they, Israel, and the rest of the world, will see it! How, by Satellite, TV.—**_SHALT,_** a determined incident! The word S-H-A-L-T, means something that has to be done, and there is no other way.

Their Armour is not as it was in Ezekiel's day, for modern policemen, use Shields, and bullet proof vests, and other means of protection.

*[17] "Thus saith the Lord GOD; Art thou he of whom I have spoken in old time by my servants the prophets of Israel, which prophesied in those days many years that I would bring thee against them?"*

Ezekiel might not have known, about what he was writing, but he wrote as the Lord spoke it to him, he didn't have to know, all he had to do was to write as God dictated it to him.

*[18] "And it shall come to pass at the same time when Gog shall come against the land of Israel, saith the Lord GOD, that my fury shall come up in my face."*

The use of the words the Lord GOD, means a title of Majesty and great power, Almighty God.

It seems there ought to be a bunch of Exclamations, at the end of this verse, because God fierce anger comes up, or vengeance, which means Anger with a Vengeance!!!!!

The next few verses indicates, a nuclear bomb of some kind, perhaps an Hydrogen bomb, which will kill humans any where within a certain mileage radius, and not harm, jeeps, tanks, trucks, etc. Because when we come to the **_39ᵗʰ_** **_chapter_** it says, that he will send fire on Russia, and the isles, that dwell carelessly .

This writing, will not have to be dreaded by born again believers in Christ Jesus, but some lost persons might read this and take warning, at least that is my prayer, that before the rapture of the church, and the lost will be left behind, and doomed to hell, and the Lake of fire .

*Revelation 6:1—8—[1]* *"AND I saw when the Lamb opened one of the seals, and I heard as it was a noise of thunder, one of the beasts saying, Come and see."*
*[2] "And I saw, and behold a white horse: and he that sat on him had a bow; and a crown was given unto him: and he went forth conquering, and to conquer." (Anti-christ)*
*[3] "And when he had opened the second seal, I heard the second beast say, Come and see."*
*[4] "And there went out another horse that was red:(Russia) and power was given to him that sat thereon to take peace from the earth, and that they should kill one another and there was given unto him a great sword."*

(Most likely an Hydrogen Bomb was this great sword, that John saw)

*[5] "And when he had opened the third seal, I heard the third beast say, Come and see. And I beheld, and lo a black horse; and he that sat on him had a pair of balances in his hand."*

And when a war of this magnitude is waged, it will cause a world wide famine, that is what the balances represent, scales, if you will, everything will be rationed, because of this war.

This is when the Mark of the beast comes into play, this is the only way people will be able to buy, or sell. Unless they have this mark in their foreheads, or on their right hand.

*[6] "And I heard a voice in the midst of the four beasts say, A measure of wheat for a penny, and three measures of barley for a penny; and see thou hurt not the oil and the wine."*
*[7] "And when he had opened the fourth seal, I heard the voice of the fourth beast say, Come and see."*

*[8] "And I looked and saw a pale horse: and his name that sat on him was death, and hell followed with him. And power was given unto them over the fourth part of the earth, to kill with the sword, and with hunger, and with death, and with the beasts of the earth."*

One fourth of the population of the earth at this time will be wiped out, death, on every hand, a great famine, and because of the famine, people will starve to death, and the beasts of the earth will kill many people, because of their hunger, and of course, those people will go to hell, because they refused the truth, of the gospel, and decided, they didn't need any kind of religion, especially, not Christianity. That kind of religion is too easy to receive, all a person has to do is to ask for it. If it were by works, then many more would receive it, but it is too easy.

*Ezekiel 39:6 "And I will send a fire on Magog, and among them that dwell carelessly in the isles: and they shall know that I am the LORD."*

Nuclear warheads, no doubt, on nations that dwell carelessly, and an Isle, is an unknown nation of Ezekiel's time, remember always God knows, but to explain to Ezekiel, would probably take years to make him understand. From verse 17-to the end of this chapter, the scene moves forward, to the battle of Armageddon, compare it with *Revelation 19ʲ 17,18*.

*Revelation 19:17,18—[17] "And I saw an angel standing in the sun; and he cried with a loud voice; saying, to all the fowls that fly in the midst of heaven, Come and gather yourselves together unto the supper of the great God;"*
*[18] "That ye may eat the flesh of kings, and the flesh of captains, and the flesh of horses, and of them that sit on them, and the flesh of all men, both free and bond, both small and great."*

Now don't mistake the battle of Armageddon, with the war that we are talking about in *Ezekiel, 38,39,* for they are entirely different wars.

The difference *is that one sixth of this army* will be left alive and return to their home. WHY? Because there has to be many folks after the reign of Christ, to fulfill his word once again. most of the Arab nations, will be destroyed along with the others because they will ally their selves, to destroy Israel.

*Ezekiel 39:2* *"And I will turn thee back, and leave but the sixth part of thee, and will cause thee ro come up from the north parts, and will bring thee upon the mountains of Israel."*

Almighty God is still working in the hearts of man, even though man, or least most of mankind, refuses to believe in God, but one thing for sure, is that God will see to it that his word never fails, his word will be fulfilled.

After this war is finished, the nation of Israel will take over the temple mount, as a result of the Hydrogen bomb, the temple mount top most likely, will be destroyed, and the Israelis will rebuild the temple mount, and the Beast will make a covenant with Israel according to Daniel, for one week and in the middle of that week, he will break that covenant, that's in the middle of the Great Tribulation period.

*Daniel 9:27* *"And he shall confirm the covenant with many for one week: and in the midst of the week ha shall cause the sacrifice and the oblation to cease, and for the overspreading of abominations he shall make it desolate, even until the consummations, and the determined shall be poured upon the desolate."*

In the middle of the seven years, the beast will declare himself to be God, and demand worship from all the people, and this is when Jesus told Israel to flee to the mountains,

*Matthew 24:15-23* *"When ye therefore shall see the abominations of desolation, spoken of by Daniel the prophet, stand in the holy place, (whoso readeth, let him understand)"*
*[16] "Then let them which be in Judaea flee into the mountains:"*
*[17] "Let him which is on the house top not come down to take any thing out of his house:"*

*[18] "Neither let him which is in the field return back to take his clothes."*

*[19] "And woe unto them that are with child, and to them that give suck in those days!"*

*[20] "But pray ye that your flight be not in the winter, neither on the sabbath day:"*

*[21] "For then shall be great tribulation, such as was not since the beginning of the world to this time, no, nor ever shall be."*

*[22] "And except those days should be shortened, there should no flesh be saved: but for the elect's sake those days shall be shortened."*

*[23] "Then if any man shall say unto you, Lo, here is Christ, or there: believe it not."*

Remember, when I repeat some verses of scripture, it is to make a certain point.

This is when the Beast breaks his covenant with Israel, and demands people to worship him, also this is when Isaiah warns Israel, and others who will refuse to recognize the beast(Anti-christ) as the Messiah to flee to the mountains of Moab.

*Isaiah 16:4 "Let mine outcasts dwell with thee, Moab: be thou a covert to them from the face of the spoiler for the extortioner is at end, the spoiler ceaseth, the oppressors are consumed out of the land."*

This is where the people that will be saved, will hide for three years and six months, and the beast can't touch them, and according to Daniel, these three countries will escape out of the hand of the Anti-christ.

*Daniel 11: 41 "He shall enter also into the glorious land, and many countries : shall be overthrown : but these shall escape out of his hand, even Edom, and Moab, and the chief of the children of Ammon."*

These three countries of Edom, Moab, Ammon in Old Testament times, are found, in which is now modern day Jordan. And then, When the Lord returns, in his second event of his second coming, at the end of the Great Tribulation Period of Seven years, or better than that, seven years after the Rapture of the Church, and he will come back to Israel, by way of Bozrah, (Edom, the land of Esau) which is also found in modern day Jordan. This is where the Remnant of Israel will be and the remnant of Egypt, and the remnant of Assyria. hiding from the Anti-christ, or the beast, for after the Beast, sets himself up in the Temple, and demands worship, then the last half of the Seven Year Tribulation, will be the time of God's wrath on wicked mankind, and God will hide his people from his own wrath, and God will hide Israel, and the remnant, of Egypt, and the Remnant of Assyrians, from the Anti-christ, and from the devil, you see, God even tells all, who will listen where he will hide his people, and the devil, who knows the scriptures, can't touch them, because of God's Divine Protection.

*Isaiah 63:1-6—[1]* *"WHO is this that cometh from Edom, with dyed garments from Boz-rah? This that is glorious in his apparel, travelling in the greatness of his strength? I that speak in righteousness, mighty to save."*
*2. "Wherefore art thou red in thine apparel, and thy garments like him that treadeth in the winefat?"*
*[3] "I have trodden the winepress alone; and of the people there was none with me: for I will tread them in mine anger, and trample them in my fury; and their blood shall be sprinkled upon my garments, and I will stain all my raiment."*
*[4] "For the day of vengeance is in mine heart, and the year of my redeemed is come."*
*[5] "And I looked, and there was none to help; and I wondered that there was none to uphold: therefore mine own arm brought salvation unto me; and my fury, it upheld me."*
*[6] "And I will tread down the people in mine anger, and make them drunk in my fury, and I will bring down their strength to the earth."*

This happens approximately seven years after the Rapture of the church, and The Church will go to stand before the Judgment seat of Christ, and when the Judgment seat of Christ is over, then

Christ Jesus, will present his bride to his Father, and then, will be the Marriage of the Lamb, and the Marriage supper.

But the war we are talking about, happens here on this earth, approximately seven years, before he returns to fight the battle of Armageddon, Immediately after the rapture of the church.

You see, the events that will take place, by the Beast, and, will even fool two thirds of the nation of Israel, and they will receive the mark of the beast, and doom their souls to hell, but, One third will refuse the mark of the beast, and God will hide them in the land of Modern day Jordan, from the face of the Anti-christ, and the place where you can find this recorded is found in,

*Zechariah 13:8,9—[8] "And it shall come to pass, that in all the land, (Israel) saith the LORD, two parts therein shall be cut off and die; but the third shall be left therein."*
*[9] "And I will bring the third part through the fire, (Tribulation) and will refine them as silver is refined, and will try them as gold is tried: they shall call on my name, and I will hear them: I will say, It is my people: and they shall say, The LORD is my God."*

There are seventy weeks of years, determined on the children of Israel, and these weeks will be fulfilled, and the acts of the Beast, in the first half of the Seven years of Great Tribulation Period, will be so great, that all those who will refuse Salvation of the Lord during the Church age, will accept the mark of the beast, because he will come in peace, so, he says, and will do great wonders, in the earth, that all the lost will accept him as being the Messiah, you see, the devil, is a mocker, Whatever God does, the devil will attempt to do it, and don't think, that the devil doesn't know the scriptures, for he surely does, and he always attempts to be equal with the Lord God, but he only fools those who want to be fooled, if not they would have accepted the Lord Jesus Christ as their Saviour, when they had the chance to do so.

*Daniel 9:24 "Seventy weeks are determined upon thy people and upon thy holy city, to finish the transgression, and to make an end of sins, and to make reconciliation for iniquity, and to bring in everlasting righteousness, and to seal up the vision and prophesy, and to anoint the most Holy."*

Let me stop here and attempt to explain, these verses of scripture, he says that there are **Seventy Weeks** Determined on the children of Israel, and these are years, and today we are in-between, the **69ᵗʰ week**, and the **Seventieth week** of years, the seventieth week will be the Seven years of the Great Tribulation Period, from the time of the commandment by Cyrus the Persian, to go back and restore the temple, and the city of Jerusalem, until, the Lord's Crucifixion, there are 69 weeks, and because Israel refused to accept the Messiah, the Lord turned to the Gentile nations, to win a bride for Christ Jesus, and now we are in between the 69ᵗʰ week, and the 70ᵗʰ week, so to explain this, from the Commandment of Cyrus the Persian, for Israel to go back home and restore the Temple, and the walls, and the city of Jerusalem, in Ezra's and Nehemia time, when Cyrus sent them back to restore the walls of Jerusalem, and Ezra to restore the Temple in Jerusalem, until the crucifixion of Christ Jesus, was 690 years, then God turned to the Gentiles, and when the bride of Christ is finally won, then the Rapture will happen, that is when the 70ᵗʰ week begins, which is seven years, and the total years will be 697 years determined on Israel to make an end to sins.

***Daniel 12:4-7—[4]*** *"But thou, O Daniel, shut up the words, and seal the book, even to the time of the end; many shall run to and fro, and knowledge shall be increased."*
*[5] Then I Daniel looked, and behold, there stood other two, the one on this side of the bank of the river, and the other on that side of the bank of the river*
*[6] And one said to the man clothed in linen, which was upon the waters of the river, How long shall it be to the end of these wonders?"*
*[7] "And I heard the man clothed in linen, which was upon the waters of the river, when he held up his right hand and his left hand unto heaven, and sware by him that liveth for ever that it shall be for a time, times, and an half; and when he shall have accomplished to scatter the power of the holy people, all these things shall be finished."*

***Time, 1 year, Times 2 years, and and one half, of a year, total, three and one half of a years.*** In the first three and one half years, of the Great Tribulation Period, he will scatter the power of the holy people, which is Israel, two thirds of the nation of Israel will accept the anti-christ, as the Messiah, and one third will refuse him as being the Messiah., AGAIN, you will find this in

**Zechariah 13:8,9—[8]** *"And it shall come to pass, that in all the land, (Israel) saith the LORD, two parts therein shall be cut off and die; but the third shall be left therein."*
*[9]And I will bring the third part through the fire, and will refine them as silver is refined, and will try them as gold is tried: they shall call on my name, and I will hear them: I will say, It is my people: and they shall say, The LORD is my God*

As I said, I will, and I have repeated some scripture, to keep them fresh in your mind, and I will repeat my comments, probably more than once, and it means, that I want to keep my comments fresh in your mind also, and I pray that I do not confuse anyone with my comments, or with the scriptures that I use in this Commentary, for my job is to enlighten, and not put the blinders on anyone.

And these verses found in Zechariah, tells us that the beast, or anti-christ will accomplish to scatter the people of Israel, not from the nation, of Israel, but from one another, scatter their belief, now those who accepts the anti-christ as god, will be doomed, and beside all that, the one true God of heaven and earth, knew who would accept the anti-christ, as being the Messiah they have been looking for, for so long, and he also knew who would refuse the anti-christ, as being the Messiah, even before the foundation of the world.

The anti-christ, will embody every evil known to man, and then some, but he will be a very good persuader, because he will persuade two thirds of the entire nation of Israel, that he is the Messiah, that they have been looking for so many years, when he rescues Israel, from this mighty force that comes against them, this Russian led mob of soldiers, from most every nation in the world, but God is going to protect Israel, even if he has to use the devil to do it.

There is a replacement theory, and that means, that the Church, has replaced Israel, and that God will never deal with Israel again, but that is a lie, of Satan, for God has said, that he only turned his back on Israel, for a moment, Israel is now God's people, and he will save a remnant of Israelis, during the last half of the Great Tribulation period, and the 144,000, is one tenth of the remnant, of Israelis, that will be saved. If you multiply 144,000 x10 it = 1,440,000, that is one million four hundred & forty thousand Israelis that will be saved, plus, 1,440,000 Egyptians, and 1,440,000, Assyrians which is a total of 4,320,000, that will be saved during the Great Tribulation period, Four Million, three hundred, and twenty thousand .

And many people are deceived by, misinterpretation of scripture————————————————-.

**_Revelation 7:9_ *"After this I beheld, and, lo, a great multitude, which no man could number, of all nations, and kindreds, and people, and tongues, stood before the throne, and before the Lamb, clothed in white robes, and palms in their hands."***

And you might protest, that this multitude came out of great tribulation, and they did, but this multitude is before the throne of God while the Seven years of Great Tribulation, is going on here on this earth, and every child of God does go through great tribulation here on this earth, for the devil, is trying every one who is born again, constantly, day and night, ever since, they trusted the Lord to save their soul.

Ever since the time of Adam, and Eve, the people of God, have been in great tribulation, because the devil hates God, and he hates anyone that belongs to God, therefore the devil, will and has done everything he can do, to hurt God's people, in the attempt to destroy the work of God, in this world. And anyone, who is a child of God, must know this.

While the apostle John saw this multitude, that no man could number, he was looking on the earth, also he was looking at the Throne of God, in heaven, where this multitude, was gathered, praising God the Father, and the Lord Jesus Christ. And if you will notice, they were from every nation, and from every kindred, and people, and tongues, this could only describe the church, as well as, the Old Testament saints, they were already clothed with white robes, meaning the church had already been before the Judgment

Seat of Christ, and received their rewards, also the Old Testament Saints, will be clothed in white robes.

Even today, I heard on the news, that our current President, wants to not test our Nuclear weaponry, anymore, but is talking about signing a Nuclear agreement, with Russia, and according to the Past, Russia, will still test their Nuclear power, and where will that leave the USA?

Our Nuclear Weaponry, is one thing that has held back the Russian forces, from attacking our Allies, because they think, that it would cause too much damage to the country of Russia, but I also know, that all in all it is not yet the Time, on God's Timetable, but I truly believe that a nuclear war is on the Horizon, with the USA, and the Russian led Army, with the thoughts of doing away with Israel, in order to gain their riches, riches in gold, and silver, as well as the riches of the Dead Sea.

Israel is under attack, even now, the number of rockets that have been fired upon Israel in 2010, is 191, and Rockets are again raining on Israel in southern Israel, from the Gaza strip, and they are furnished by Iran, Iran is massively funding anti-Israel global English and Spanish language TV stations to mask their nuclear aims; also top leaders are questioning the centrality of Jerusalem to the Jewish people also I received this via E-mail, Iran-backed Hezbollah is rearming at massive levels in Lebanon; Anti-Israel activity on campus is harming the future, and, most importantly, the US-Israel relationship is under siege, and Americans must do all we can to support Israel.

It's been two years since Thanksgiving attacks in India because of their ties, to Israel, these two countries are united in the attempt to prevent terrorism these countries relationship has galvanized the cooperation, and attacks have resulted in improved corporations in a Varity of sectors.

Washington, November 24- in the two years since the Mumbai massacres, ties between Israel and India have strengthened as the two countries have joined forces to fight Islamic extremist and protect against future attacks. On November 26/2008, the day after Thanksgiving, 10 extremist from a Pakistan-based terrorist group killed more than 170 people and wounded more than 300 others, Including Hindus,. Jews, Christians, and Muslims, in attacks on two luxury hotels, a train station, a café and other sites.

The terrorists assaulted the city's Jewish center, killing six people, including four Israelis, the only surviving perpetrator, Ajmal Kasab, told police they targeted Israelis to avenge the atrocities on Palestinians. The news media, is only making things worse in Israel-Palestinian negotiation, in trying to work out a peaceful solution because of their anti-Israel stance.

*Zechariah 12:1-3—[1] "THE burden of the word of the LORD for Israel, saith the LORD, which stretcheth forth the heavens, and layeth the foundation of the earth, and formeth the spirit of man within him."*
*[2] "Behold, I will make Jerusalem a cup of trembling unto all the people round about, when they shall be in the siege both against Judah and Jerusalem."*
*[3] "And in that day will I make Jerusalem a burdensome stone for all people: all that burden themselves with it shall be cut in pieces, though all the people of the earth be gathered together against it."*

This is what the Lord is telling us, He said no matter how many people of the world come against Jerusalem, and Judah, I will protect it, I will take care of my people.

*The following is an E-mail, that was sent to me, back in October 11/2010, and it is titled, Iran expands international Media outlet, and it is all anti-Israel content/ based in Tehran, Press TV maintains offices throughout the world. Republic news agency (IRNA) overtly supports Hezbolliah, as Press TV's content is more subtle, Programs are centered on U.S. foreign policy and the middle east, particularly Israel and the Palestinians. It also has a sister company, Atlantic Television news, based in Denmark and with an office in downtown Washington, D.C. Media outfit, highlights direct statements from Hezbollah leader Hassan Nasrallah . Refrences to the U.S. -Israel relationship are frequent, particularly those questioning the two countries ties. Iran-backed Hezbollah's news -long established channel, Al-Manar, stresses its ties to Iran, and its support for attacks against Israel. Al-Manar was launched in 1991 and is a mass outlet, calling itself the "Station of resistance" against Israel. Al-Manar is the preferred outlet for Palestinian groups claiming responsibility for terrorist attacks against Israelis. It is a popular Lebanese news site that broadcasts images of Hezbollah fighters in addition to glorifying attacks on Israel. The United States and Germany banned the station due to its incitement of terrorist activity. Al-Manar also promotes Iranian President Mahmoud Ahmadinejad as a friend of Lebanon and touts his upcoming visit to Lebanon on Oct. 13,14, (Remember I received this October 10/2010/)*

*Al-Manar's web site states, The visit is the first of its kind, and therefore is exceptional and significant . That's why Hexbollah and AMAL movement called on Lebanese for wide participation in the reception of the "Great Guest"—Ahmadinejad's visit to Lebanon has garnered full official interest on the country's internal scene as Prime-Minister Saad Hariri is expected to hold a luncheon banquet in his honor. Hezbollah-controlled southern suburb, Harat Hurayk. The poor, conservative, Shi'ite neighborhood takes direction from Nasrallah. As opposed to other Lebanese news stations closed down for violation of Leban's law against propaganda, Al-Manar enjoys the tacit support of Beirut and Damascus in addition to Tehran. Muslim communities in Europe, Canada, and the United States provide funding through large donations to Al-Manar. They also appeal for donations and solicit funds under Hezbollah's name as well as "The Intifada in occupied Palestine Fund" "The Palestine uprising and" "The Resistance Fund." in 2004, reports revealed most of the male reporters were gurrilla fighters before joining Al-Manar. Funding also comes from Hezbollah's business ventures located in Beirut, south Lebanon, and Bekaa Valley. Enterprises include heavy machinery and drug trafficking. One headline from "Islamic Republic news agency,— " Why does the U.S. let Israel get away with having nuclear Arsenal?"*

___*Today March 23/2011,*___ I received this via E-mail, from Christians united for Israel, and the following is what is stated————————————————,

"Today, Israel's enemies have spoken. And they have spoken loudly. Terrorists have detonated a bomb at a crowded bus stop near the Jerusalem Convention center, the blast killed one woman and injured over thirty additional individuals. It's a miracle there weren't more fatalities. Earlier in the day, terrorists in Gaza fired two Katyusha rockets at the southern city of Be'er Sheva and a barrage of mortar shells on the western Negev. over the course of the last week, terrorists fired over 50 rockets into Israel's southern towns and cities. We can respond to these attacks on Israeli civilians with anger and with loss of hope, but it is far better to respond with action. As Israel's enemies act, so must we. In particular, we must grow Christians United for Israel bigger, and stronger, so that we can speak out in defense of Israel more effectively than ever."

*This points to the soon stirring, of Israel's enemies, to start this war, we have been talking about, and it's building, and building, until it finally, comes into fruition.*

*By Rex Jones Evangelist/ teacher/ of the gospel / all scripture used in this commentary. is, from, the authorized King James Version. Except where I attempt to let you know, that you can't trust every thing that says, it's a bible. The Authorized King James Bible has been proven, over and over, that it is God's holy Word, to the English speaking people.*